THE

CW00794326

AESTHETIC MOVEMENT

IN ENGLAND

THE

AESTHETIC MOVEMENT

IN ENGLAND

BY

WALTER HAMILTON

Fellow of the Royal Geographical and Royal Historical Societies;
Author of "The Poets Laureate of England," "A History of National Anthems and
Patriotic Songs," "A Memoir of George Cruikshank," &c.

"Have you not heard how it has gone with many a cause
before now? First, few men heed it; next, most men contemn
it; lastly, all men accept it -- and the cause is won."
William Morris

London
Pumpernickel Press
2011

First published by Reeves and Turner, London, in 1882.

This reprint of the third edition first published by
Pumpernickel Press in 2011.

Pumpernickel Press
Office 3512
PO Box 6945
London
W1A 6US
United Kingdom

Aside from instances where errors
in the original text render the content too
difficult to read, the original spelling, grammar and
punctuation are used throughout.

ISBN-13: 978-0-9559796-8-2

PREFACE TO THE THIRD EDITION

THE agreeable duty of preparing a new edition of this little work (which has met with support an approval beyond its merits and my expectations), has been rendered doubly pleasurable from the kind assistance which has been voluntarily tendered by many gentlemen whose names are prominently connected with the movement I have endeavoured to describe.

In dealing (however superficially), with the lives and works of many eminent men now living, or but recently passed away, a few errors in facts or dates were inevitable; these have been corrected with the utmost care. The chapter on the late Dante Gabriel Rossetti has been rendered much more complete by the insertion of interesting information kindly supplied me by his brother, Mr. William Michael Rossetti; and I have also borrowed a few notes from Mr. T. Hall Caine's *Reminiscences of Dante Gabriel Rossetti*, a work which I can heartily commend to all who take an interest in the career of that singular man of genius, and the great artistic movement he originated.

The Earl of Southesk has favoured me with some notes about his curious poem, *Jonas Fisher*; and to Lady Wilde I am greatly indebted for the very complete account I am enabled to offer of the career of her son, Mr. Oscar Wilde, about whom, at present, considerable curiosity exists, both at home and in the United States.

For other valuable assistance I beg to offer my grateful acknowledgements to the Rev. T. W. Carson, of Dublin; Mr. F. W. Crawford; and Mr. Jonathan Carr, of Bedford Park. Nor has their friendly assistance benefited me only, it has enabled me to offer the public a more complete, and more authentic account of the Aesthetic Movement than has yet been written, and to correct many misapprehensions which have existed concerning its origin and its aims.

I have used the title Aesthetic Movement, little as I like it, because it is generally accepted and understood, although it incorrectly describes what might be more correctly styled, a Renaissance of Mediaeval Art and Culture.

WALTER HAMILTON.

64 Bromfelde Road, Clapham,

London.

CONTENTS

INTRODUCTION

A SHORT time since two very favourite theatres were drawing large audiences to witness, in the one case a comic opera, in the other a comedy, written with the avowed purpose of ridiculing a certain school, known as the Aesthetic.

Satire and ridicule are legitimate weapons when directed against shams, hypocrisy, or any other species of humbug, and dramatists or the comic journals simply perform a public duty by pointing the finger of scorn at anything that is false, or ignoble. But of all the thousands who crowded to see *Patience* and *The Colonel*, how few there were who carried away any distinct idea of the actual meaning of the satires they contained; or who could form any clear opinion as to whether the class of persons therein held up to ridicule were actually existing literary and artistic men, or simply the creations of the fertile pens of a couple of dramatists, who had taken hints from a journal which had, at one time, some claim to the title of a *comic* paper.

But supposing a small percentage of the theatre-goers to have traced a resemblance between the dramatic characters and the Maudles, Postlethwaites and Company, of the aforesaid comic paper, the question would still arise, as to whether Maudle, Postlethwaite and Company were purely imaginary individuals, or were living and walking in our midst, and so grossly deceiving the world with a sham Art, Poetry, and Criticism, as to deserve to be subjected to the scorn and derision of all people of intellect and education, and to find their pictures, poems, and essays laughed out of the market, and themselves reduced to live in the unromantic humdrum manner of ordinary civilized beings.

But the fact is, that Maudle and Company, as portrayed, were not altogether imaginary individuals, but belonged to a comparatively new school, which has done, and is still doing, an immense amount of good towards the advancement of Art in this country and in America. That there are persons of Aesthetic tastes who carry them to the borders of absurdity goes without saying; every movement in intellectual, or political, life has its over-enthusiastic apostles, who damage the cause they have at heart; but that there must be *some* good in the movement is clearly shown by its having earned the abuse of a journal which never has a generous word to say for any one beyond its own immediate and narrow circle. However, the so-called Aesthetic School has now been in existence some years, and is likely to survive the attacks which a portion of the press levels at it, the more so because by far the greater number of its assailants neither study its works, understand its aims, nor appreciate the undoubted good it has wrought.

What then, is this school, - what are its aims, - and what has it achieved?

The term Aesthetic is derived from the Greek, *aisthesis*, signifying *perception*, or the science of the beautiful, especially in art, and the designation has long been applied by German writers to a branch of philosophical enquiry into the theory of the beautiful, or more accurately, into the philosophy of poetry and the fine arts. The term appears to have been invented, or adopted, by Baumgarten, a German Philosopher, whose work entitled *Aesthetica* was published in 1750.

A great controversy has been going on in Germany for a century and a-half, the chief topic in dispute being the question as to whether an object is actually beautiful in itself, or merely

9

appears so to certain persons having faculties capable of appreciating that which is *positively* beautiful.

From this dispute came the origin of the school, and the Aesthetes are they who pride themselves upon having found out what is the really beautiful in nature and art, their faculties and tastes being educated up to the point necessary for the full appreciation of such qualities; whilst those who do not see the true and the beautiful - the outsiders in fact - are termed Philistines.

Now up to a certain point, the theory that beauty is apparent only to some, is perfectly sound, for most persons will agree with Kant, that there can be no strict mathematical definition, or science of beauty in nature, art, poetry or music, inasmuch as beauty is not altogether a property of objects or sounds, but is relative to the tastes and faculties brought to bear upon them.

Illustrations of the truth of this axiom will occur to every one; it is founded upon the old old truism, *tastes differ*, The Aesthetes recognise this truth to the fullest extent, but having first laid down certain general principles, they have endeavoured to elevate taste into a scientific system, the correlation of the arts being a main feature of the scheme; they even go so far as to decide what shall be considered beautiful, and those who do not accept their ruling are termed Philistines, and there is no hope for them.

Hence, the essence of the movement is the union of persons of cultivated tastes to define, and to decide upon, what is to be admired, and their followers must aspire to that standard in their works and lives. Vulgarity, however wealthy it may be, can never be admitted into this exclusive brotherhood, for riches without taste are of no avail, whilst taste without money, or with very little, can always effect much. So also those who prate most of Aestheticism are often those who have least of it to show in their houses, furniture, dress, or literary culture.

It has been insinuated that the school has no existence, save in the brain of M. Du Maurier, or that if it existed, it was yet merely a very insignificant clique of nobodies, whose vanity was gratified by the attention thus called to them, and to their paltry works. But the school does exist, and its leaders are men of mark, who have long been at work educating public taste, hence *Punch* found it to its interest to ridicule it, and parody its works; when the topic was worn thread-bare in its pages, the editor appropriated a plot from a French play, took his situations from an old comedy called *The Serious Family*, worked in the stale jokes of his journal, and so produced his new, original, and most successful *Colonel*.

For more than twelve months this *rechauffé* drew crowded houses, but in the height of its much advertised successful career, it was taken off the boards, somewhat suddenly and inexplicably, a few days after the publication of the first edition of this work, in which its origin was distinctly traced, and its *animus* explained.

It was certainly a laughable and most amusing production; but neither for art nor originality would it bear comparison with Gilbert and Sullivan's delightful *Patience, or Bunthorne's Bride*, which was first produced at the Opera Comique, London, on Saturday, 23rd April, 1881 (although it was stated that the libretto of the opera was completed in the November preceding, some time before the production of *The Colonel*), and played continuously until the 22nd November, 1882.

By means, then, of these two plays, the Philistines were

afforded a glimpse behind the scenes, so to speak, of Aesthetic life, and had placed before them, in a highly-spiced and dangerously exaggerated form, the manners and customs of a very exclusive section of society, of whose very existence only a vague and uncertain idea had previously been formed.

Suppose, then, as it is a matter of curious philosophical interest, that we take a few steps back into the past, to discover the origin of the Aesthetic Movement, note the characteristics of its founders and their principal followers, the development of the school, and the influence it has exercised over modern art and poetry.

THE PRE-RAPHAELITES

IN the year 1848 there were studying together in the art school of the Royal Academy, four very young men, namely, Holman Hunt, John Everett Millais, Dante Gabriel Rossetti, and Thomas Woolner, the first three being painters, the last a sculptor. Associated with these artists were two young literary men, William Michael Rossetti and F. G. Stephens, both art critics, and the late Mr. James Collinson. This small band of seven constituted the Pre-Raphaelite Brotherhood. Endowed with great originality of genius, combined with remarkable industry, they formed amongst themselves the daring project of introducing a revolution into the arts of poetry, painting and sculpture, as then practised in England.

But 1848 was fertile in Revolutions!

These youths were enthusiastic in their admiration of early Italian art and the mediaeval Pre-Raphaelite painters, and they christened themselves the Pre-Raphaelite Brotherhood. In the earlier period of the movement they even signed their works with the initials "P. R. B." [1]

---

[1] Several examples of this practice were found amongst the effects of the late D. G. Rossetti, and were thus enumerated in the catalogue of the sale held last July :-

"The following items were presented to Dante G. Rossetti towards the beginning of the Pre-Raphaelite Movement, 1848:

341o. W. H. Deverell, inscribed by Rossetti, "James II. robbed by Fishermen, while escaping from England," Indian ink. A very characteristic and humorous design of this promising young artist, mounted.

341p. W. Holman Hunt, inscribed, "William Holman Hunt, P. R. B.

1848. W. Holman Hunt, to his P. R. B., Dante G. Rossetti," also by Rossetti, "One Step to the Deathbed (Shelley), by W. H. Hunt."

341R. J. E. Millais, R. A., "Two Lovers. The Lady's Dress caught by the Thorns of a Rosebush" (intended for Keats' Isabella,) inscribed by Millais, "P. R. B. J. E. Millais, 1848, John E. Millais to his P. R. Brother Dante Gabriel Rossetti," and by Rossetti, "J. E. Millais." Indian ink outline, framed.

It was suggested that they should all reside together, and curiously enough the house they particularly had in view was the very one in which Dante Gabriel Rossetti did eventually reside, namely, 16, Cheyne Walk, Chelsea. One member proposed that a door-plate should be provided, with the letters "P. R. B." engraved upon it, but W. M. Rossetti pointed out that profane or jocular persons might read it as "Please Ring the Bell," so that idea was abandoned, and eventually the whole scheme was given up, as it failed to meet the varying requirements, and means, of the several members.

In 1850 they started a Pre-Raphaelite Magazine, entitled *The Germ*, of which William Michael Rossetti was appointed editor.

The pictures contributed by the P. R. Brotherhood to the Royal Academy in 1849 were highly spoken of, and in the following year an article in the *Illustrated London News* first explained in print the signification of the magic initials P. R. B., giving some gossip about the men who composed the society, and the purposes they had in view. This disclosure caused a great stir amongst the critics and connoisseurs of the art world, and abuse was freely poured upon the new persuasion, as might have been expected.

Mr. Ruskin, however, came to the rescue of the persecuted

youths (Millais, the most prominent, being only 21 at the time), and in a letter to The Times, and also in a pamphlet entitled *Pre-Raphaelitism*,[2] took up arms on their behalf. He thus explains his motives in the preface - "Eight years ago, in the close of the first volume of 'Modern Painters,' I ventured to give the following advice to the young artists of England :-

'They should go to nature in all singleness of heart, and walk with her laboriously and trustingly, having no other thought but how best to penetrate her meaning; rejecting nothing, selecting nothing, and scorning nothing.'

"Advice which, whether bad or good, involved infinite labour and humiliation following it; and was therefore, for the most part, rejected.

"It has, however, at last been carried out, to the very letter, by a group of men, who, for their reward, have been assailed with the most scurrilous abuse which I ever recollect seeing issue from the public press. I have, therefore, thought it due to them to contradict the directly-false statements which have been made respecting their works; and to point out that kind of merit which, however deficient in some respects, those works possess beyond the possibility of dispute."

He sums up the errors made about their works thus - "These false statements may be reduced to three principal heads, and directly contradicted in succession."

"The first, the current fallacy of society, as well as of the press, was, that the Pre-Raphaelites imitated the *errors* of early painters."

"A falsehood of this kind could not have obtained credence

---

[2] *Pre-Raphaelitism*. Smith, Elder & Co., 1851.

anywhere but in England, few English people, comparatively, having ever seen a picture of the early Italian masters. If they had, they would have known that the Pre-Raphaelite pictures are just as superior to the early Italian in skill of manipulation, power of drawing, and knowledge of effect, as inferior to them in grace of design; and that, in a word, there is not a shadow of resemblance between the two styles. The Pre-Raphaelites imitate no pictures; they paint from nature only. But they have opposed themselves as a body, to that kind of teaching before described, which only began after Raphael's time; and they have opposed themselves as sternly to the entire feeling of the renaissance schools - a feeling compounded of indolence, infidelity, sensuality, and shallow pride. Therefore they have called themselves Pre-Raphaelite. If they adhere to their principles, and paint nature as it is around them, with the help of modern science, with the earnestness of the men of the thirteenth and fourteenth centuries, they will, as I said, found a new and noble school in England. If their sympathies with the early artists lead them into mediaevalism or Romanism, they will, of course, come to nothing. But I believe there is no danger of this, at least for the strongest among them."

"There may be some weak ones, whom the Tractarian heresies may touch; but if so, they will drop off like decayed branches from a strong stem."

"I hope all things from the school."

"The second falsehood was, that the Pre-Raphaelites did not draw well. This was asserted, and could have been asserted only by persons who had never looked at the pictures."

"The third falsehood was, that they used no system of light and shade. To which it may be simply replied that their system of light and shade is exactly the same as the sun's, which is, I believe, likely to outlast that of the Renaissance, however brilliant."

"They are different in their choice, different in their faculties, but all the same in this, that Raphael himself, so far as he was great, and all who preceded or followed him who ever were great, became so by painting the truths around them as they appeared to each man's own mind, *not as he had been taught to see them*, except by the God who made both him and them."

He then proceeds to describe the distinct attributes, and in several cases to warmly commend, the works of John Everett Millais, William Hunt, Samuel Prout, John Lewis, Mulready, and Edwin Landseer, whilst also devoting much space and eloquent praise to the works of J. M. W. Turner.

In 1850 the Illustrated London News gave an engraving of Millais' picture, "Christ in the Carpenter's Shop," of which it remarked :-

"This picture is painted, it is said, on a wrong principle, but with a thousand merits and many intentional defects. What is called somewhat slightingly the Pre-Raphaelism of this picture is its leading excellence. The intentional deformities are not at all to our taste, but the picture has so many merits that all its eccentricities may be very well excused, though they cannot be overlooked."

And when in 1852 Millais exhibited his famous picture, "The Huguenot," the tide of public opinion turned completely in his favour, and the critics found themselves unable to withstand the popular verdict of approval.

Of the P. R. Brotherhood itself, henceforth little more was heard, and of its seven members, only one, Holman Hunt, has remained faithful to his original creed, and he has won a high position in his art, taking as much as £10,000 for a single picture (alas! that art and £ s. d. should have to come in such juxtaposition), and having had the proud satisfaction of refusing to become a Royal Academician.

Woolner, after some rough experiences at the gold fields in Australia, returned to England, became professor of sculpture at the Royal Academy, and has executed some fine statues of our great public men.

Millais has long since reached the summit of his profession, a result for which he has to thank the good taste of the British public far more than the sapient art critics, who seldom recognise genius until it is too late for their praise to be of use. Neither of these three famous artists is, however, to be actually identified with the present Aesthetic Movement, and indeed, in the magnificent residence of Millais, at Palace Gate, Aestheticism is conspicuous by its absence, and no Aesthetic poet dedicates sonnets to him. When, however, we come to the fourth of the original members of the Pre-Raphaelite Brotherhood, Dante Gabriel Rossetti, now perhaps more widely appreciated as a poet than as a painter - his poems are accessible, his principal paintings are hidden from the public gaze in private collections - in him we find that union of the artistic faculties which is held to constitute a true Aesthete developed to the fullest extent, and indeed he must be held the foremost member of a school which mainly relies upon the correlation of the arts.

And if he were not the actual founder of the school, his genius and admitted abilities, both in poetry and painting, rendered him a typical representative of the movement, in which the combination of the two arts is constantly aimed at, the one being held to be the complement of the other. A generation earlier, the eccentric poet-artist Blake had attempted something similar, but without much success, although his poems, illustrated by his own hand, now fetch very high prices, owing doubtless to Swinburne's enthusiastic praise of them in his "Critical Essay on William Blake,"[3] which is in every way worthy of his pen - strong and vigorous in style, and truly poetical in sentiment.

In an address delivered at the Social Science Congress at Manchester, in 1879, Sir Coutts Lindsay tersely described the aims of the Pre-Raphaelites, and the results of their labours. In his remarks about the various sections or groups into which English painters might be classified, he said :-

"One of these groups originated the so-called Pre-Raphaelite Movement. The epithet is an unmeaning one, but, as it is generally applied and accepted, it is sufficient. The influence of this group of men has been felt far and wide, and has impressed the imagination of the public in a very remarkable manner.

---

[3] The biography of this extraordinary man has been well written by Alexander Gilchrist (assisted by the two Rossettis), in 1863, but those who wish to obtain a real insight into the genius and spirit of his work must peruse Swinburne's magnificent essay.

William Blake was born near Golden-square, on 20th November, 1757, and died in poverty in August, 1827, in dismal lodgings in a close off the Strand. He was apprenticed to Basire, an engraver; but in addition to his work as an engraver, Blake produced a number of poems, in which the text and designs were interwoven, and it is upon these singular works that his fame now rests.

The *Jerusalem* is the largest and most important, and in the weird variety of its illustration the most marvellous of Blake's productions. Of the others, the principal are "The Marriage of Heaven and Hell"; "The Book of Thel"; "Milton"; "Songs of Innocence and Experience"; "America" and "Europe". In 1782 he married Catherine Boucher, who survived him about four years. When she died she was buried at the side of her well-loved husband, but where that was there is no monumental stone to tell, so little was Blake prized by his contemporaries.

"I pointed out when speaking of Reynolds, that English painters were, during his time, under subjection to the Italian and Dutch schools, and dependent on a class of men wedded to scholastic ideas; the result being the abandonment of the knowledge derived from Nature, and a narrow dogmatism based on what are called the canons of art.

"I said that a school of painting, founded on such a basis, must narrow more and more with age, and must end by producing dead conventionalities instead of living truth. I pointed out, however, that our school was gradually shaking itself clear of these influences, and I mentioned some among many painters whose labours were adding fresh lustre to our school, long before the Pre-Raphaelites were heard of. Yet, there is doubt, that there still continued a strong taint of conventionality and falsehood in the practice of our art, and the Pre-Raphaelite Movement was the result.

"Half-a-dozen young men set themselves to the reconsideration of art - the outcome of their thought appeared to them a revelation, and the consequence a mission.

"They worked with the zeal and fanaticism of religious enthusiasts. Their creed involved the denial of everything the English school had hitherto held sacred. They accepted Nature alone to be their future guide and Bible, and in it they beheld the condemnation of all art *except the earliest art of Italy.*

"These men threw themselves passionately into the study of the natural, and had implicit faith in the all-teaching of Nature without assistance from the stores of past knowledge.

"They soon became the observed of all observers, and the accepted prophets of the hour. They produced a number of most interesting works, replete with excellence and truth on the one side, whilst wanting in the first principles of art in the other.

"Holman Hunt, Millais, Burne-Jones, Rossetti, and several others, were the apostles of this movement. You are probably acquainted with their early works, and also with what they do now. Their present works are the best proofs of how their faith has enlarged and their knowledge deepened with time.

"Painting and poetry are nobly blended in the efforts of these men."

THE GERM

I HAVE already alluded to a small magazine started by the Pre-Raphaelite Brotherhood, having for its chief raison d'être, the union of art and letters in one harmonious whole. *The Germ* was, in fact, to be written by artists and poets for the benefit of artists and poets, and though, for some tolerably obvious reasons, the magazine did not succeed, it had several features of interest especially considered in relation to the rising Aesthetic School - for its chief contributors have since become identified with that movement - whilst nearly every name originally connected with the unsuccessful little literary venture, has since become famous in art or letters.

Only four parts were published; the first in January, 1850, the last in April of the same year, and the price was one shilling.

"THE GERM,

"Thoughts towards nature in Poetry, Literature, and Art."

Such was the title-page of Parts 1 and 2; Parts 3 and 4 were slightly altered, thus :-

"THE GERM,

"Being thoughts towards Nature. Conducted principally by artists."

The title on some copies appears to have been afterwards altered to *Art and Poetry*.

On the wrapper of each part appeared the lines :-

"When whoso merely hath a little thought

Will plainly think the thought which is in him,

Not imagining another's, bright or dim,

Not mangling with new words what others taught;

When whoso speaks, from having either sought

Or only found - will speak, not just to skim
A shallow surface with words made and trim,
    But in that very speech the matter brought:
Be not too keen to cry - 'So this is all!
    'A thing I might myself have thought as well,
'But would not say it, for it was not worth!'
    Ask, 'Is this truth?' For is it still to tell
That, be the theme a point, or the whole earth,
    Truth is a circle, perfect, great or small?"

At the end of the first and second parts appeared this announcement :-

"THE GERM.

"This Periodical will consist of original Poems, Stories to develop thought and principle, Essays concerning Art and other subjects, and Analytic Reviews of current Literature - particularly of Poetry. Each number will also contain an Etching; the subject to be taken from the opening article of the month.

"An attempt will be made, both intrinsically and by review, to claim for Poetry that place to which its present development in the literature of this country so emphatically entitles it.

"The endeavour held in view throughout the writings on art will be to encourage and enforce an entire adherence to the simplicity of nature; and also to direct attention, as an auxiliary medium, to the comparatively few works which Art has yet produced in this spirit. It need scarcely be added that the chief object of the etched designs will be to illustrate this aim practically, as far as the method of execution will permit; in which purpose they will be produced with the utmost care and completeness."

"On the third and fourth parts the advertisement was

differently worded :-

ART AND POETRY.
BEING THOUGHTS TOWARDS NATURE.
Conducted principally by Artists.

"Of the little worthy the name of writing that has ever been written upon the principles of Art (of course, excepting that on the mere mechanism), a very small portion is by Artists themselves; and that is so scattered that one scarcely knows where to find the ideas of an Artist except in pictures.

"With a view to obtain the thoughts of Artists upon Nature, as evolved in Art, in another language besides their *own proper* one, this Periodical has been established.

"Thus, then, it is not open to the conflicting opinions of all who handle the brush, and palette, nor is it restricted to actual practitioners; but is intended to enunciate the principles of those who, in the true spirit of Art, enforce a rigid adherence to the simplicity of Nature either in Art or Poetry, and consequently regardless whether emanating from practical Artists, or from those who have studied Nature in the Artist's School.

"Hence this work will contain such original Tales (in prose or verse), Poems, Essays, and the like, as may seem conceived in the spirit, or with the intent, of exhibiting a pure and unaffected style, to which purpose analytical Reviews of current Literature - especially Poetry - will be introduced; as also illustrative Etchings, one of which latter, executed with the utmost care and completeness, will appear in each number."

An accordingly each of the four parts was illustrated by an etching of a decidedly Pre-Raphaelite appearance. The first, by W. Holman Hunt, illustrates "My Beautiful Lady," a poem by Thomas Woolner (since re-published by Macmillan in 1863). The second by James Collinson, represents the child Jesus; the third and largest by F. Madox Brown, is a scene from King Lear, which is accompanied by a short poem entitled "Cordelia," by Wm. M. Rossetti; the fourth, by W. H. Deverell, is an etching entitled "Viola and Olivia," it is certainly the least pleasing of the series, and the three verses with it (by J. L. Tupper) have little merit.

Of the other contents, the most prominent appear to have been an article by F. Madox Brown, "On the Mechanism of a Historical Picture"; "O, When and Where," a pretty little poem by Woolner; "The Blessed Damozel," by Dante Gabriel Rossetti; the latter being the poem which, when it was long afterwards republished, Mr. R. Buchanan took occasion to criticise as follows :-

"The nearest approach to a perfect whole is the "Blessed Damozel," a peculiar poem which appeared in a rough shape many years ago in *The Germ*, an unwholesome periodical started by the Pre-Raphaelites, and suffered, after gasping through a few feeble numbers, to die the death of all such publications. In spite of its affected title, and of numberless affectations throughout the text, the 'Blessed Damozel' has merits of its own, and a few lines real genius. - (R. Buchanan." *The Fleshy School of Poetry*).

D. G. Rossetti's other poems in *The Germ* were "The Carillon," "From the Cliffs," and six sonnets on various pictures.

Then there was an article on Macbeth by Coventry Patmore, and several other poems and articles signed by D. G. Rossetti, Christina G. Rossetti,[4] Thomas Woolner, James Collinson,

---

[4] This talented lady, the authoress of numerous poems, is the youngest of the Rossetti family, having been born in 1830; William Michael was born in 1829; Dante Gabriel in May, 1828; whilst the eldest, Maria Francesca, who was born in 1827, died in 1876; she wrote a somewhat noted work entitled, *A Shadow of Dante*.

Ellen Alleyn, John Seward, Calder Campbell, Walter H. Deverell, Laura Savage, and W. B. Scott. Ellen Alleyn was, in fact, only a *nom de plume* adopted by Christina G. Rossetti, whilst F. G. Stephens assumed the pseudonyms John Seward and Laura Savage. There was also a long article entitled "A Dialogue in Art," the author of which Mr. John Orchard, had recently died, says a note, which further explains that he had not been very successful as an artist.

The last article of all is a review of Robert Browning's poem, "Christmas Eve and Easter Day." This, written by W. M. Rossetti, the editor, is a keen analysis of Browning's peculiar and involved style; Rossetti admits he is metaphysical, complicated, and obscure, but he adds - "Surely if you do not understand him the fact tells two ways. But if you *will* understand him, you shall."

We cannot expect all poets to write in the simple, child-like style of a Wordsworth or a Longfellow, and when a man of genius, as Browning undoubtedly is, writes a poem, or Wagner composes an opera, it is at least worth while to try to discern the beauties they contain before we pronounce an opinion against them.

It pleased Mr. Buchanan, in his attack on the Pre-Raphaelites and Aesthetes, to stigmatise *The Germ* as an *unwholesome* publication. Blind prejudice, or absolute ignorance of its contents, might explain, but could scarcely excuse such a statement. The magazine was written by men for men, and not for school missis in simpers and curl papers. It was frank and bold, but unwholesomeness existed only in the mind of him who went to seek it. Prophetic in its title, it was before its time; its aims were not understood; the circle to which it appealed was too small; but *The Germ* was there, whence a great and beautiful tree of art has since sprung up.

This little work is now exceedingly rare, and as it contains early writings of men who are now widely celebrated it is much sought after, and five pounds is no unusual price for what originally cost but four shillings.

For some time after the death of *The Germ*, the Pre-Raphaelites were the objects of ridicule and misrepresentation; but they continued to work on patiently in their various arts, in which before long nearly every one attained eminence, and truly some of their success was due to the powerful writings of John Ruskin, who from the first had discerned how much there was of the beautiful and true in the new style inaugurated by the P. R. B.

JOHN RUSKIN

A FEW words here about this eccentric genius. A native of London, born in February, 1819, John Ruskin went to Christ Church, Oxford, where he distinguished himself as the winner of the Newdigate prize for English verse in 1839,[5] and four years later he produced the first volume of his greatest work, "Modern Painters," which at once brought him prominently before the artistic world, and since then his reputation as the greatest authority on art, and the first critic of the age, has been firmly established. His keen analysis of the ideas which should govern *art*, his clear definitions of the really true and beautiful, and above and before all, his eloquent and forcible denunciations of all shams and of the modern cheap-Jack styles of architecture, pictures, and literature, these are of world-wide celebrity; but, unfortunately, he has occasionally descended from the throne on which he reigns supreme, to mix in the troubled strife of the noisy rabble who prate and squabble on the vexed questions of political economy. Being unused to hear his *dicta* on art questioned, he has also expected that his views on political economy would equally be accepted without cavil, and has shown no little chagrin when his facts have been disputed and his conclusions disproved.

To this dislike of contradiction must be added a kind of irritable pessimism, which not only makes him bitterly dissatisfied with things as they are, but causes him at times to rail

---

[5] *"Salsette and Elephanta,"* a Prize Poem. Recited in the Theatre, Oxford, June 12, 1839, by John Ruskin, Christ Church.

against those who would wish honestly to ameliorate them, and to despair of any real improvement being practicable; least of all unless the *initiative* has been of his taking.

Such being his well-known opinions, and his style of expressing them being often of a more forcible than courteous description, it is no wonder that the following letter obtained a wide credence.

At the distribution of prizes to the art classes at Chesterfield in November, 1880, the secretary read an extraordinary communication purporting to come from Mr. John Ruskin, in answer to one asking him to give them a lecture. It was as follows :-

"Harlesden, London, Friday.

"My dear Sir, - Your letter reaches me here. I have just returned from Venice, where I have ruminated in the pasturages of the home of art; the loveliest and holiest of lovely and holy cities, where the very stones cry out, eloquent in the elegancies of Iambics. I could not if I would go to Chesterfield, and I much doubt whether I would go if I could. I do not hire myself out - after the fashion of a brainless long-tongued puppet - for filthy ducats. You, and those who told you to write me, want me, I presume, to come that you many make money for your art class; and if I should get you much money, you will then tolerate some good advice from me. No, I will not come.

"I have heard of Chesterfield. Hath it not a steeple-abomination, and is it not the home - if not the cradle - of that arch abomination-creator Stephenson? To him are we indebted for the screeching and howling and shrieking fiends fit only for a Pandemonium, called locomotives, that disfigure spots of God's own land.

29

"I will not come to Chesterfield. Tell your students that art is a holy luxury, and they must pay for it. Tell them to study, to ponder, and to work with a single thought for perfection, observing loving and strict obedience to the monitions of their teacher. Let them learn to do things rightly and humbly, and then, by the conviction that they can never do them as well as they have been done by others, they may be profited.

"My good young people, this is pre-eminently the foolishest - yes, quite the foolishest - notion that you can get into your empty little egg-shells of heads; that you can be a Titian, or a Raphael, or a Phidias; or that you can write like Seneca. But because you cannot be great, that is no reason why you should not aspire to greatness. In joy, humility, and humbleness, work together. Only don't study art because it will pay, and do not ask for payment because you study art. Art will make you all wiser and happier, and is worth paying for. If you are in debt - as I suppose you are, or why pester me? - pay off your debts yourselves. If you write to me only that you may get money, you are on the foolishest of all errands. Wisdom is more precious than rubies, and is offered to you as a blessing in herself. She is the reward of industry, kindness and modesty. She is the prize of prizes, the strength of your life now, and an earnest of the life that is to come. This advice is better than money, and I give it to you gratis. Ponder it and profit by it. - Ever faithfully yours, John Ruskin."

Many were the comments which this letter, widely published, as it was sure to be, created; for admiration of the past, and the theory, shared with Mr. Carlyle, that people are "mostly fools," had long been expressed by Mr. Ruskin, and scarcely any one doubted the authenticity of the letter addressed to Chesterfield, a name which at once recalls that of a celebrated Earl who also wrote letter, but *his* were on the art of politeness.

But a few days afterwards Mr. Ruskin denied that he had composed the epistle; it is, therefore, only of interest as so clever a parody of his style that the whole London press was deceived by it. Now lovers of literature owe so much to Mr. Ruskin that it is almost painful to comment on his too frequent expressions of petulant prejudice. Mr. Ruskin's writings, "The Stones of Venice," "The Seven Lamps of Architecture," "Modern Painters," and many of his quaintly-named minor works, have as it were, given eyes to the blind. They have widened the circle of the nobler pleasures, and even when they excite opposition, teach people to think and see for themselves. As an essayist on other topics Mr. Ruskin has done one great service. He has kept telling our age that we are not precisely "the roof and crown of things," and he has made us acknowledge that in olden times people did many noble things better than we can do them.

Mr. Ruskin's numerous works are not readily accessible, for he has peculiar ideas with regard to their publication, refusing to re-issue some of his writings in order not to depreciate the value of those in the hands of present possessors of the early copies. Thus, many of his pamphlets and essays command prices quite out of proportion to those at which they were issues. Whilst by not having a London publisher, the book-selling and book-buying public in general have not been so well informed about his writings as they would have been had the books been generally exhibited for sale in the usual manner.

Mr. George Allen, of Orpington, Kent, sends out a list of Mr. Ruskin's works to intending purchasers, accompanied by the following :-

31

ADVICE BY MR. RUSKIN.

I have directed Mr. Allen, in this and all future issues of his list of my purchasable works, to advertise none but those which he is able to dispatch to order by return of post. The just estimate of decline in the energy of advancing age, - the warnings, now thrice repeated, of disabling illness consequent on any unusual exertion of thought; - and, chiefly, the difficulty I now find in addressing a public for whom, in the course of the last few years of Revolution, old things have passed away, and all things become new, render it, in my thinking, alike irreverent and unwise to speak of any once-intended writings as "in preparation."

"I may, perhaps, pray the courtesy of my readers, - and here and there, the solicitude of my friends, - to refer, at the time of the monthly issue of Magazines, to this circular of Mr. Allen's, in which, on the terminal page, they will always find the priced announcement of anything I have printed during the month. May I also venture to hint to friends who may at any time be anxious about me, that the only trustworthy evidences of my health are my writings: and that it is a prettier attention to an old man, to read what he wishes to say, and can say without effort, than to require him to answer vexing questions on general subjects, or to add to his day's appointed labour the burden of accidental and unnecessary correspondence."

John Ruskin, and E. Burne-Jones (to whom Swinburne dedicated a volume of his poems), have been sometimes named as belonging to the original P. R. Brotherhood, but erroneously it appears.

Ruskin, as before mentioned, only became identified with

the "P. R. B.,' through taking up the cudgels against the press on its behalf, he being then a young man.

It seems, however, that on the dissolution of the original brotherhood, a number of enthusiastic admirers set to work to imitate it, and whilst copying all the eccentricities of the real, original, and only Pre-Raphaelites, appeared to be ignorant of the fact that they wanted the genius of those who set the movement a-foot.

This Whistler (the "Impressionist"), whose name is frequently quoted with that of Burne-Jones, as a representative of the extreme section of the school (although, indeed, the two artists have little in common), is so far unfaithful to the creed of the original "P. R. B." that we find him bringing an action against John Ruskin, the quondam champion of that body.

Ruskin had vindicated Turner from the attacks of those who were able to see the eccentricity only, and not the genius of that artist, of those who thought his work but

"A landscape, - foreground golden dirt,
The sunshine painted with a squirt."

Ruskin clearly demonstrated that Turner, in spite of his peculiarities, knew and painted more of nature than any other artist that ever lived, but at the same time he was not prepared to go the length of praising the absurd parodies of Turner's style then being produced in almost any number, and dignified by such appellations as symphonies in black and yellow, or harmonies in green and gold, many of which pictures not only the public but even the art critics could not decipher. Amongst Ruskin's numerous critical articles, there was one in which he sharply rebuked Mr. Whistler, whose mannerisms were then the talk of the whole artistic world. The critic had said of the artist that he flung a paint-pot in the face of the public, and called it a picture. Hence the law-suit, Whistler *v.* Ruskin. This action was an amusing episode in the history of painting, and the result showed the folly of appealing to a prosaic British Jury on a question of pretended transcendental art. It was said at the time of the prolific manufacturer of arrangements, symphonies, nocturnes, and harmonies, in gold and silver, that he was reduced to making a composition in whitewash with his creditors, as he became bankrupt shortly after receiving his verdict for a farthing damages.

Nothing daunted with the small result he had obtained at law, Mr. Whistler had recourse to the pen, and published a pamphlet on *Art and Art Critics*, which had a very considerable sale. He takes the very natural stand, "that one might admit criticism from a man who had passed his whole life in the science which he attacks."

He shows how a critic had written in the *Times*, of June, 1864, that "a picture was slovenly in execution, and poor in colour," which, as it afterwards appeared, was a Velasquez, and had revelled in the praises of a supposed Turner, that was shown not to be a Turner at all. What, he asks, should we think of the Observatory at Greenwich under the direction of an apothecary, or the College of Surgeons with Tennyson as President? "Yet a school of art, with *littérateur* at its head, disturbs no one. What greater sarcasm can Mr. Ruskin pass upon himself that that he preaches to young men what he cannot perform! Why, unsatisfied with his conscious power, should he choose to become the type of incompetence, by talking for forty years of what he has never done!"

There is much that is reasonable in this, and it is easy to

call to mind a dozen instances in which the critics have been wrong, and the public in the right. The virulent attacks made upon the early works of Shelley, Keats, Byron, and Tennyson, will occur to every one. But in this particular instance public opinion seemed to side with Ruskin, for people were beginning to tire of pictures which looked quite as well upside down as any other way, and when Mr. Edward Terry (as *Pygmalion Flippit*, an artist of the Future) produced his "Dual Harmony," in the amusing little comedy called *The Grasshopper*, all London crowded to see his picture, which represented the boundless blue ocean beneath a burning sky, or if reversed, showed the vast sandy desert under a blue and cloudless one. And the merry laughter over his simple red and blue picture probably had more effect in discrediting these ridiculous travesties of art than all Mr. Ruskin's powerful articles. These incidents call to mind the usual remark of unsuccessful men, especially artists; that popularity mainly results from chance or fashion, and is no proof of real genius.

And, when all is said, it must be remembered that Mr. Ruskin is, after all, little more than an art critic and a literary man - he is not an *artist*, and Mr. Whistler in his pamphlet has some remarks on this point which are worthy of recollection.

"The war," he says (referring to the action, "Whistler v. Ruskin") "fought the other day in Westminster, is really one between the British and the Pen, and involves the absolute *raison d'être* of the critic. To the cry on their part, 'that they must live,' I reply at once, 'I do not see the necessity.' Over and over again did the Attorney-General cry out loud, 'What is to become of painting if the critics withhold their lash?' As well might he ask, what is to become of mathematics under similar circumstances, were they possible. We are told that Mr' Ruskin has devoted his long life to art, and as a result is Slade Professor at Oxford. A life passed among pictures makes not a painter. As well might one allege that he who lives in a library must needs become a poet. The Attorney-General said, 'There are some people who would do away with critics altogether.' I agree with him, and am one of those he points at; but let me be clearly understood - the *art* critic alone would I extinguish. That *writers* should destroy *writings* to the benefit of *writing* is reasonable. But let art work be received in silence, as it was in the days to which pen-men still point as an era when art was at its apogee. Harm the critics do, and not good. Furnished as they are with the means of furthering their foolishness, they spread prejudice abroad; and through the papers at their service, thousands are warned against the work they have yet to look upon."

Nor is it English artists alone who have occasion to complain of the ignorance and incompetence of the critics. The early life of the truly sublime artist, Antoine Wiertz, was embittered by his strife with the arrogant wasps of the French and Belgian press.

The art criticisms of Victor Joly have long since faded into oblivion, but his features, as preserved by Wiertz in his caricature "Don Quiblaque" will never be forgotten when once seen. Wiertz had also his revenge by collecting all the contradictory *dicta* from the various criticisms, and republishing them side by side, an extraordinary jumble of almost incredible imbecility being the result. And again, when after years of toil and anxiety, his glorious "Patroclus" obtained admission to the Louvre and was faintly praised by a few Parisian critics, he affixed the following satirical note, which may still be traced on the left-hand side of that *magnificent chef* d'oeuvre now in the Wiertz Museum at Brussels :-

"Nous, Feuilletonistes de Paris, Princes de la critique, seuls reconnus souverains et garantis infaillibles. A nos bons et fidèles vassaux les critiques d'Allemagne, ceux d'Angleterre, ceux de Belgique qui se nourissent de bière, etc., etc.; les dits bons critiques le sont assez pour ne reconnaitre d'autres Lois que celles emmanées de nos plumes, et voulant venir en aide aux dits bons critiques appelés a formuler un jugement sur le present ouvrage de peinture:-

"Avons appliqué au dit ouvrage le sceau de notre approbation Parisienne."

"Donné a Notre Exposition du Louvre le 15 Août, 1844."
(Here is a seal consisting of a carrot and a peacock's feather crossed, with the legend "approbation Parisienne.") Wiertz laboured hard to prove that painters knew more of art than did the critics, a proposition not difficult of demonstration, and yet how largely is the public mind influenced by the anonymous articles of irresponsible, and often incapable, critics, who would write with equal pomposity and assurance on Chinese metaphysics, a game of cricket, Moltke's strategy, or the integral calculus.

But Mr. Whistler may surely expect the millennium to come about before art criticism is abolished, and as any one who *considers* he has "taste," also *considers* himself equal to pronouncing a judgement on works of art, we must leave the public to discriminate between the true and the false in criticism.

Now, although Ruskin chose to speak out plainly in the matter of Mr. Whistler's pictures, there is no doubt but that the *true* Aesthetic School owes much to him, not only for pointing out the real direction in which pure art and real beauty are to be found, but also for a style of phraseology, forcible and picturesque in itself, but which, unfortunately, easily lends itself to burlesque and absurd exaggeration.

Let us take a small extract from his notes on Samuel Prout and William Hunt's loan collection of pictures.

"That little brown-red butterfly [142]... is a piece of real painting; and it is as good as Titian or anybody else ever did, and if you can enjoy it you can enjoy Titian and all other good painters; and if you can't see anything in *it* you can't see anything in *them*, and it's all affectation and pretence to say that you care about them. And with this butterfly in the drawing I put first, please look at the mug and loaf in the one I have put last of the Hunt series, No. 171. The whole art of painting is in that mug - as the fisherman's genius was in the bottle. If you can feel how beautiful it is, how ethereal, how heathery, and heavenly, as well as to the uttermost muggy, you have an eye for colour and can enjoy heather, heaven, and everything else below and above. If not, you must enjoy what you can contentedly, but it won't be painting; and in mugs it will be more the beer than the crockery, and on the moors rather grouse than heather."

For those who have neglected the opportunity of testing their taste for art on this butterfly, and on this mug, I would advise a visit to Venice, to learn whether they can appreciate Bassano's hair trunk, as shown in his grand picture of the Pope Alexander and the Doge of Venice. It is *not* Ruskin, but one who has read Ruskin who thus describes it :-

"The hair of this trunk is real hair, so to speak, white in patches, brown in patches. The details are finely worked out; the repose proper to hair in a recumbent and inactive condition, is charmingly expressed. There is a feeling about this part of the work, which lifts it to the highest altitudes of art; the sense of sordid realism vanishes away - one recognises that there is *soul* here. View this trunk as you will, it is a gem, it is a marvel, it is a miracle. Some of the effects are very daring, approaching even to the boldest flights of the rococo, the sirocco, and the Byzantine schools. Yet the master's hand never falters - it moves on, calm, majestic, confident; and, with that art which conceals art, it finally casts over the *tout ensemble*, by mysterious methods of its own, a subtle something which refines, subdues, etherealizes the arid components, and endues them with the deep charm and gracious witchery of poesy. Among the art-treasures of Europe there are pictures which approach the hair trunk - there are two which may be said to equal it, possibly - but there is none that surpasses it."

It is thus that Mark Twain pleasantly parodies Ruskin's language, and at the same time, deprecates the custom of critics who go into raptures over a worthless picture or statue, because it happens to be old, damaged, and worm-eaten, and can see no merit in the productions of to-day.

It seems strange that in these days when democratic sentiment is so far spreading in every direction, that the artist alone, be he painter, sculptor, musician, or poet, should proclaim aloud, his *odi profanum vulgus*. Yet 'tis but a short time since the gifted, and essentially-popular, President of the Royal Academy, Sir Frederick Leighton, who has little if any sympathy with the extreme Aesthetic School, thus adopted their mode of speaking in an address to a society of architects :- "So long as there exists amongst the public a grotesque indifference to beauty, and a callous indifference to ugliness - until the people have a higher sense and a more refined perception of beauty, the career of the true architect will be, I fear, a life-long struggle against the solid, and serried ranks of the Philistines."

39

Now Ruskin, we know, always writes in this way. This in his criticism of Miss. Thompson's pictures, which he ends by praising enthusiastically, he premises by saying, "but I had thought that what the public admired must be bad," and many amusing examples of this kind of writing are to be found in his books and articles.

So, too, in the musical world, we find Wagner (who, by the way, has many points in common with our Aesthetic School) displays a similarity contemptuous regard of public opinion.

If this want of appreciation really exists to the extent these supercilious artists and authors would have us believe, the remedy is with them; to educate the public taste up to the required level they have but to put before the public nothing but works of the purest, noblest, and most refined artistic merit; flashy mediocrity, and fleshly drivel will shortly then be banished from our walls and book-shelves.

THE GROSVENOR GALLERY

BUT to return to our Aesthetes. It was by the foundation of Sir Coutts Lindsay's Grosvenor Gallery a few years ago that strength and solidity were first given to the movement amongst the artists of the school. They thus obtained a head quarters for their art, and the founder was one of themselves in his opinions. Although nothing can take from the venerable Royal Academy its historical prestige, yet it has certainly found a formidable rival in the Bond-street gallery.

Pictures are admitted to the former institution *nominally* by selection according to merit; but in the Grosvenor Gallery the more exclusive system has been adopted of *inviting* artists to exhibit. This method of admission has enabled painters who were either unwilling (as many were) or unable to obtain an *entrée* into the Royal Academy, to bring their best works prominently before the general public, without having to run the gauntlet of jealousy of the Royal Academicians, and without having to bow down before a narrow-minded and exclusive *clique*, which settles not only *who* shall exhibit, but can at any time punish an unpopular man by placing his work so high, or so low, that only a giant or a child can catch a glimpse of it.

Those who have regularly visited the Grosvenor Gallery cannot fail to have noticed the characteristics of the Aesthetic School, as represented in the pictures exhibited there since 1878.

With the exception of the numerous paintings of J. A. Whistler, whose works have principally been noted for the affected titles bestowed upon them, the pictures are noticeable for the prominence given in them to the union of the arts of poetry and painting, their topics being frequently selected from the works of the poets of the Aesthetic School; they are next remarkable for the skill and care bestowed upon the colouring, the tints usually being of a subdued, often a sombre nature, as more suited to the weird and mournful character of many of the compositions.

A weird sort of sensation of being carried back into the Middle Ages is engendered by long gazing at these pictures, for in that temple of art of which Burne-Jones is the high priest, one seems to feel the priestly influence stealing over one, as when standing before some piece of glorious glass-painting in and old Gothic cathedral. Indeed, the resemblance is somewhat more than fanciful, for in these compositions the figures are strongly defined, clearly detached, and transparent in tint, and the effect is very similar to that seen in stained glass windows.

Perspective does not seem to have received the same amount of attention as colour; and this, coupled with the somewhat constrained and angular attitudes of the figures, a peculiar arrangement of closely fitting draperies, and the general tone of colours employed, give the majority of the paintings an appearance which can best be indicated as resembling the Japanese style of art, a resemblance which is also to be found in the furniture and costumes adopted by people of Aesthetic tastes.

But it is in the portrayal of female beauty that Aesthetic art is most peculiar, both in conception as to what constitutes female loveliness, and in the treatment of it.

The type most usually found is that of a pale distraught lady with matted dark auburn hair falling in masses over the brow, and shading eyes full of love-lorn languor, or feverish despair; emaciated cheeks and somewhat heavy jaws; protruding upper lip, the lower lip being indrawn, lone crane neck, flat breasts, and long thin nervous hands.

It naturally follows that artists having selected this ideal of loveliness, certain ladies should endeavour to attain it, and in not a few cases they have earned the derision of the Philistines, one of whom thus describes :-

A FEMALE AESTHETE.

"Maiden of the sallow brow,
Listen whilst my love I vow!
By thy kisses which consume;
By thy spikenard-like perfume;
By thy hollow, parboiled eyes;
By thy heart-devouring sighs;
By thy sodden, pasty cheek;
By thy poses, from the Greek;
By thy tongue, like asp which stings;
By thy zither's twangy strings;
By thy dress of stewed-sage green;
By thy idiotic mien;-
By these signs, O aesthete mine,
Thou shalt be my Valentine!"

Edward Burne-Jones, Dante G. Rossetti, and James MacNeill Whistler have already been mentioned as artists of the Aesthetic School, but there are many others whose works have received quite as much attention, and are quite as Aesthetic in their style.

I will enumerate a few only of the *more characteristic* paintings recently exhibited in the Grosvenor Gallery, which will serve to show how widespread has been the influence of the movement,

and how ridiculous it is to sneer at the results it has achieved.
E. Burne-Jones - "Laus Veneris."

> "Le Chant d'Amour."
> "Pan and Psyche."
> "The Annunciation."
> "The Golden Stairs."
> "The Mill."
> "Danae at the Brazen Tower."
> "The Tree of Forgiveness"

All these are indeed pictures of the most intense and romantic stye, "Laus Veneris" was painted 1873-75, and it must be remembered that many years before that, Swinburne had dedicated his poem, having the same title, to E. Burne-Jones, as this is a most interesting link in the Aesthetic idea of the union of the arts of poetry and painting.

"Pan and Psyche" also represents an incident taken from another poem, William Morris's "The Earthly Paradise."

"The Tree of Forgiveness," which worthily occupied the position of honour in this year's Grosvenor Exhibition, was a remarkable picture, full of the highest poetical inspiration, and most intense in its expression of love and sorrow.

"Phyllis, amidst her mourning because Demophoon had forsaken her, was turned by the kind gods into an almond tree; and after, as he passed by, consumed with sorrow for her, she became once more visible to him, no less loving then of old time; and this was the first blossoming of the almond tree."

The apparition of the lovely Phyllis springing forth from the trunk of the almond tree, and almost as it were out of he picture, has a powerful and startling effect, the anatomy of the limbs being brought into powerful relief, whilst the deep despair and yearning of heartfelt love depicted on the faces long dwell on the memory.

J. M. Strudwick. - "Marsyas and Apollo."

"Peona." From Keats's "Endymion."

"Saint Cecilia."

"Isabella."

"Passing Days."

Sir Coutts Lindsay, Bart. - "Ariadne."

"The Fates."

"The Boat of Charon."

Cecil G. Lawson. - "The Minister's Garden."

"In the Valley."

"The August Moon."

"The Voice of the Cuckoo."

This talented artist, who died in June last, at the early age of 30 years, has left works which show that he could treat landscapes so as to bring out the poetical, as well as the artistic beauties of nature, suggestive as well as imitative. His style was bold an firm, and his colouring vivid; his death has deprived the world of an artist of great promise.

In this year's exhibition at Grosvenor were three landscapes by him, and one painting, entitled "Provence Roses," by his wife.

Of his, perhaps "The Storm Cloud" was the most characteristic, being a study of somewhat gloomy mountain scenery, with heavy masses of moving storm clouds. The others were a view on the road to Monaco, and "September," a wild sunset effect, with some cattle half seen through autumnal haze.

C. Fairfax Murray. - "A Pastoral."

This curious Pre-Raphaelite picture represented ten richly

clad figures seated near a wood in a glow of sunlight, listening to one playing.

W. E. F. Britten. - "Che Sara Sara."

G. P. Jacomb Hood. - "Una."

R. Spencer Stanhope. - "The Shulamite."

Especially Pre-Raphaelite in arrangement.

L. Alma Tadema. - "A Torch Dance."

A very singular and powerful work.

Walter Crane. - "The Fate of Persephone."

"That fair field,
Of Enna, where Proserpine, gathering flowers,
Herself a fairer flower, by gloomy Dis,
Was gathered." - *Paradise Lost.*

"The Sirens."

"Europa."

"Truth and the Traveller."

"Man sought for Truth, and cried, 'Where dost thou dwell?'
A thousand tongues replied, but none could tell.
He seeks no more; the very stones declare,
And Truth sits naked by the wayside well."

Also a wonderfully conceived and exquisitely coloured picture in this year's gallery of an Angel stopping the hand of Fate.

"Would but some winged angel, ere too late,
Arrest the yet unfolded roll of Fate,
And make the stern recorder otherwise
Enregister, or quite obliterate!"

James A. M. Whistler. -

The names of a few only of the works of this prolific artist can be given, but enough to show the eccentric affectation he displays in the selection of his titles - an affectation which has probably brought down upon him more ridicule than all the adverse opinions of the critics would have done.

"Arrangement in black and white,"

"Harmony in blue and yellow."

"Nocturne in grey and gold."

"Variation in flesh colour and green."

"The Gold Girl." (Miss Connie Gilchrist.)

"The Pacific; harmony in green and gold."

"Note in blue and opal." Jersey.

"Scherzo in blue." A portrait of a girl in blue.

But why a Scherzo? Certainly Mr. Whister's picture does not make one wish to see them often, either in Nature or Art; whilst some of the other paintings make one wish one could clearly see anything at all in them, as in his nocturne in black and gold, and nocturne in blue and silver, both of which one may study closely without perceiving any drift in the compositions, through the mist which overlays them.

It may be urged that the Aesthetic idea of the correlation of the arts is carried to an absurd extent, when Mr. Whistler borrows musical terms for titles for his paintings, but the eccentricities of his nomenclature are as nothing compared with the peculiarities of his style of execution. That he *can* be a powerful painter, capable of broad, bold effect, is fully evidenced by the portraits he occasionally exhibits; as, for instance, that of Mrs. H. B. Meux, styled "Harmony in Flesh-colour and Pink," a full-length portrait of a lady dressed in pearl-grey, relieved with broad bands of pink silk. Here, although the idea given is that the painting lacks finish and depth, it is vigorous and effective, and one can, at least, understand the artist's conception. No doubt Mr. Whistler would consider that persons who failed to grasp the poetical ideas contained in his two nocturnes - those in "Blue and Silver," and in "Black and Gold," - were wanting in perception, and these *may* be full of the deepest meaning and most exquisite beauty, but to the ordinary observer, it must be confessed, they convey no tangible idea whatever.

That there are many frequenters of the Grosvenor Gallery who talk glibly enough about this school and that, without being able to describe the most salient features of any one, is well known. This inability may - nay, generally does - arise from sheer ignorance; but it may also arise from the extreme difficulty there is of giving by word-painting a reproduction of colour-painting. It is even so with the Aesthetic School. Let anyone who is interested in the topic examine works painted by any of the artists here enumerated; he may, or may not, admire them, but he will find them generally of a poetical, romantic, sad or weird description, with colour and tone far more emblematical say, of autumnal tints, than of any other robe Lady Nature usually decks herself in. Let him then compare these works with the archly humorous conceptions of Carl Schloesser for example, instinct with life and character, and he will at once see in what the difference consists. Take the two pictures he exhibited last year, namely, "The Finishing Touch" and "The Singing Lesson;" or, better still, "An Intermezzo," a small picture in this year's Grosvenor Gallery, and if the observer have any love for art, he will be thankful that whilst Pre-Raphaelite, or Aesthetic, or Impressionist pictures are very numerous and prominent, there is still room for paintings of a more lively, and it must be confessed, of a more healthy and natural tone. Each style is charming in its turn; each serves a purpose, and each acts as a foil to show off the beauties and merits of the other.

For book illustrations the names of Walter Crane, Kate Greenaway, and R. Caldecott are justly held in high esteem, but many who admire the charming pictures produced by these artists forget that the beauty is mainly the result of the purely Aesthetic style adopted in the dresses, attitudes and surroundings of the figures.

Nor, whilst we are considering book illustrators, must J. Moyr Smith be omitted. "The Wooing of the Water Witch," "Theseus," and "The Prince of Argolis," contain hundreds of charming studies, instinct with life, beauty and delicate culture.

AESTHETIC CULTURE

FROM the consideration of the painters who are known either as Pre-Raphaelites, Impressionists, or Aesthetes, we pass naturally to the poetical division of the Aesthetic School, in which lies its principal strength, in so far as it has affected the general public and the press.

We must pause for a moment to consider what are its most prominent features and general characteristics.

First, and above all other considerations, the leaders of the Aesthetic School in poetry have been styled fleshly poets, delighting in somewhat sensually-suggestive descriptions of the passions, ornamented with hyperbolical metaphor, or told in curious archaic speech; and dressed up in quaint mediaeval garments of odd old ballad rhymes and phrases.

The strict Aesthete admires only what in his language is known as *intense*, and what Ruskin somewhat gushingly terms the "blessed and precious" in art.

Now, Henry Irving, the actor, is undeniably *intense*, and they worship him; indeed, one fair votary of the sunflower goddess was heard to remark that his left leg was a poem in itself. So also is Ellen Terry intense. She is held in the highest admiration; and Oscar Wilde, the idyllic poet (of whom more anon), after praising Irving, addresses her in the following lines :-

"I marvel not Bassanio was so bold
    To peril all he had upon the lead,
    Or that proud Aragon bent low his head,
Or that Morocco's fiery heart grew cold:
For in that gorgeous dress of beaten gold,

Which is more golden than the golden sun,
No woman Veronesé looked upon
Was half do fair as thou whom I behold.
Yet fairer when with wisdom as your shield
    The sober-suited lawyer's gown you donned,
And would not let the laws of Venice yield
    Antonio's heart to that accursed Jew -
    O Portia! take my heart: it is thy due:
I think I will not quarrel with the Bond."

He has also another ode, still more impassioned, on her assumption of the part of Camma in Tennyson's tragedy, "The Cup," itself a lovely poem which was presented to the public in a magnificent setting, as only such a priceless jewel should have.

"As one who poring on a Grecian urn
    Scans the fair shapes some Attic hand hath made.
    God with slim goddess, goodly man with maid,
And for their beauty's sake is loth to turn
And face the obvious day, must I not yearn
    For many a secret moon of indolent bliss,
    When in the midmost shrine of Artemis,
I see thee standing, antique-limbed, and stern?"

Indeed, it is at the Lyceum Theatre that Aestheticism in all its beauty can be seen. The recent revival of "Romeo and Juliet" was the most exquisite rendering of that sweet poem that has ever been presented, and although differences of opinion existed with regard to Mr. Irving's impersonation of Romeo, it was universally admitted that Juliet never had a fairer, more charming, or more talented representative than Miss Ellen Terry. Whilst as to the dresses, scenery, and grouping, they were simply perfect, and carried the mind's eye back to mediaeval Italy; indeed, every group seemed as it if has just started from the canvas of one of the early Italian masters.

So, too, in "Much Ado about Nothing," now being performed; every accessory seems perfect, every detail fitted to the place it occupies in the one grand design; whilst admirers of Irving and Miss Terry now see them in parts more suited to their ages and styles than were the youthful Romeo and Juliet.

In music the Aesthetes affect Liszt, Rubinstein, and Wagner, who are all most consummately intense.

The realism which has long since taken a firm hold of painting and poetry seem destined, ere long, to find another sphere of action in the *Opera*. Romeo and Juliet, speaking and acting as Shakespeare makes them do, have a firm hold upon our sympathies and our faith, for we all know that mortals may so have spoken and acted. But in the opera of "Romeo and Juliet" (as set forth even by such an exquisite artist as Gounod), expressing their loves and their sorrows in beautiful tunes, singing as loudly as they can over the footlights in competition with the orchestra, no longer appear artistic in any other sense than the artificial, and (*could we for a moment ignore the music*) present a spectacle as ludicrous and incongruous as does the "Traviata," who, but a moment before her death from wasting consumption, sings *bravura* passages which would sorely try the lungs of the most healthful.

This is the chasm between conventional opera and natural truth, which Wagner has attempted to bridge over.

He abandons the imbecility of making people communicate with each other in set airs, and of subordinating sense to melody to such an extent that it matters little to the audience what nonsense is sung, so long as the music is beautiful, and the voice well produced. He transfers the emotional utterances to the orchestra, and makes his personages declaim their sentiments in noble recitative, while the "motive" of each is hinted by vivid recurrent phrases from the instruments. He disuses concerted singing, only introducing an occasional chorus, under conditions which might possibly occur, such as the joyous jangling of the maiden at the opening of the third act of the *Walkyrie*, or a duet when the joint ecstasy of two individuals prompts common utterance, as in the first meeting of Siegfried and Brünhilde. He prefers myth to historical subject, for the logical reason that extraordinary and supernatural beings are not to be judged by human standards or opinion, and may properly be supposed to conduct themselves in ways which would be very inappropriate to ordinary men and women.

In painting, the Aesthetes have a great veneration for Allesandro Botticelli, a Florentine artist, who flourished about four centuries ago, and of whom Ruskin has written the praises.

It will be remembered that at the sale of the Hamilton Palace collection, last June, a picture by Sandro Botticelli was the cause of a most exciting competition. This was "The Assumption of the Virgin," painted for the Church of San Pietro Maggiore, Florence, on the commission of Matteo Palmieri. The work is on a thick panel, size 147½ inches by 89 inches. This was put up at a thousand guineas, and eventually secured by Mr. Burton, for the National Gallery, at the enormous sum of £4,777 10s.; as, however, it is unmistakably genuine, and is one of the most important examples of a somewhat rare master, it is a satisfaction to know that it is now public property. At the same sale several other works by the early Italian masters most in favour with modern Aesthetes also fetched very high prices, as, for instance, another work by Botticelli, entitled, "The Adoration of the Magi;" Giorgione's glowingly-coloured "Story of Myrrha;" an upright panel painted with figures of Vestals in monochrome, by Andrea Mantegna; and a carefully-executed portrait of a gentleman, attributed in the catalogue to Leonardo da Vinci, were all acquired for the National Gallery, at the respective prices of 1,550, 1,350, 1,700, and 500 guineas.

In architecture the Queen Anne style is favoured by the Aesthetes; and on the really beautiful Bedford Park Estate, one of the chosen homes of the "select," only houses built after this manner are permitted to be erected.

Chippendale furniture, dados, old-fashioned brass and wrought iron work, mediaeval lamps, stained glass in small squares, and old china are all held to be the outward and visible signs of an inward and spiritual grave and intensity. Let a jaded City man, if he have an eye for the beautiful, only walk three minutes off 'Change, and Dashwood House, Old Broad Street, he will find a cool, shady retreat, where he can admire at his leisure one of the finest staircases in London, decorated with a charming dado, Minton's tiles, and lit by some stained-glass windows, of exquisite colouring, put in by Pitman and Son. Or, if he can only take an hour's ride, let him visit the Sanatorium, recently built, at an enormous expense, by Mr. Thomas Holloway, at Virginia Water, and there study the decorative wall paintings, by J. Moyr Smith, especially those representing *History*, *Legend*, and *Epic Poetry*, and having studied these, let him ask himself whether such work could have been produced, or would have been appreciated, forty years ago.

Now, it cannot be too strongly insisted on that in much of

this there is visible not only a *real love of the beautiful*, but also that the wonderful improvements which have been so eagerly seized upon by the general public during the last few years originated amongst the Aesthetes, whom the vulgar herd think it witty and clever to abuse, or to ridicule. Soft draperies of quiet, sober, yet withal delicate and harmonious tints, have replaced the heavy, gaudy curtains of yore; bevelled mirrors with black frames slightly relieved with gold, have driven out the large old plates of glass, with sham, but expensive gold frames; plain painted walls, of soft tints, show up our pictures far better than the old fashioned papers which, pasted one over another, became the haunt of the agile flea, or still more objectionable but less lively insect abominations. But why the sunflower, the lily, and the peacock's feather have become so closely identified with the movement is not easy to explain; certain it is they appear to be as distinctively the badges of the true Aesthete as the green turban is amongst Mahommedans the sign that the wearer has accomplished a pilgrimage to the holy place. In these minor details, I believe the examples of D. G. Rossetti, and more recently Oscar Wilde, have had considerable influence.

Oxford, it must be remembered, was the scene of some of the first labours of the P. R. Brotherhood, and the name of nearly every distinguished member of the new school has been associated with that city. Thomas Woolner had placed a statue of Lord Bacon in the Oxford University Museum in 1856, and in 1857 Dante Gabriel Rossetti was employed to paint the frescoes in the Oxford Union Hall. In this work, although he was associated with five other artists, he was the only P. R. B. amongst them. The strange shadowy frescoes around the interior of the Union Cupola are now rapidly fading into nothingness, for the youths who painted them had no practical training in mural painting; they used no vehicle for their colours, nor did they prepare the walls to receive them, and the result has been that their interesting boyish efforts are now decayed beyond any chance of restoration. "The Oxford and Cambridge Magazine," which was in progress at the same time, contained many poems and articles by Rossetti and his friends, William Morris and Burne-Jones. This magazine ran to twelve monthly numbers; a complete set of it being of course very scarce, as all such works become immediately the public learn that they contain the early contributions of men afterwards famous. John Ruskin was a distinguished scholar and prizeman at the University, as were also A. C. Swinburne and Oscar Wilde, besides those already enumerated in preceding notes. Thus E. Burne-Jones and William Morris were undergraduates of Oxford when Rossetti was painting the frescoes in the Union, and it was mainly through his influence that they adopted their respective artistic roles.

Constantly yearning for the intense, the language of the Aesthetes is tinged with some what exaggerated metaphor, and their adjectives are usually superlative - as supreme, consummate, utter, quite too preciously sublime, &c. For some of this mannerism of speech Mr. Ruskin's writings have to answer; but the words he uses as applied to grand works of art sound ludicrous enough when debased by being applied to the petty uses of every-day small talk.

So far we have dealt with the outer characteristics - those, indeed, which being most visible, have been most ridiculed, and nowhere more cleverly that in *Patience*, where Bunthorne thus sums them up, in lines full of humour, and yet without the slightest particle of malice :-

"If you're anxious for to shine in the high Aesthetic line as a man
    of culture rare,
You must get up all the germs of the transcendental terms, and
    plant them everywhere.
You must lie upon the daisies and discourse in novel phrases of
    your complicated state of mind,
The meaning doesn't matter, if it's only idle chatter of a
    transcendental kind.
"Be eloquent in praise of the very dull old days which have long
    since passed away,
And convince 'em, if you can, that the reign of good Queen
    Anne was Culture's palmiest day.
Of course you will pooh-pooh, whatever's fresh and new, and
    declare it's crude and mean,
For Art stopped short in the cultivated court of the Empress
    Josephine.
"Then a sentimental passion of a vegetable fashion must excite
    your languid spleen,
An attachment à la Plato for a bashful young potato, or a not-
    too-French French bean!
Though the Philistines may jostle, you will rank as an Apostle in
    the high Aesthetic band,
If you walk down Piccadilly with a poppy or a lilly in your
    mediaeval hand."

And here a few words about this clever, amusing, and most
successful opera, which contrasts very favourably with its rival,
The Colonel, in being entirely original, and in the absence from
its sprightly and humorous dialogue of any tinge of personal
spite or malicious misrepresentation of the real aims of pure
Aestheticism.

The libretto of *Patience, or Bunthorne's Bride*, written by Mr. W. S. Gilbert, was completed in November, 1880, but owing to the success of its predecessor, the opera was not produced until Saturday, April 23rd, 1881, when it was played at the Opera Comique Theatre, under the personal supervision of the author, and of Mr. Arthur Sullivan, the composer of the music, which contains some of the most beautiful melodies ever heard on the English lyric stage. From that time until November, 1882, the opera was played without any interruption, although it was transferred from the Opera Comique to the Savoy Theatre on October 10th, 1881, that elegant house having just been expressly built by Mr. R. D'Oyly Carte, for the representation of Gilbert and Sullivan's pieces. On that occasion Mr. D'Oyly Carte presented an address to the public, from which I venture to quote a few paragraphs, as a short description of the theatre may be of interest to some few who are unable to visit it in person.

SAVOY THEATRE

"Ladies and Gentlemen, - I beg leave to lay before you some details of a new theatre, which I have caused to be built, with the intention of devoting it to the representation of the operas of Messrs. W. S. Gilbert and Arthur Sullivan, with whose joint productions I have, up to now, had the advantage of being associated.

"The Savoy Theatre is placed between the Strand and the Victoria Embankment, and is built on a spot possessing many associations of historic interest, being close to the Savoy Chapel, and in the 'precinct of the Savoy,' where stood formerly the Savoy Palace, once inhabited by John of Gaunt and the Dukes of Lancaster, and made memorable in the Wars of the Roses. On the Savoy Manor there was formerly a theatre. I have used the ancient name as an appropriate title for the present one.

"The new theatre has been erected from the designs and under the superintendence of Mr. C. J. Phipps, F. S. A., who has, probably, more experience in the building of such places than any other architect of past or present times, having put up, I believe, altogether 33 or 34 theatres.

"The facade of the theatre towards the Embankment and that in Beaufort Buildings are of red brick and Portland stone. The theatre is large and commodious, but little smaller than the Gaiety, and will seat 1,292 persons.

"I think I may claim to have carried out some improvements deserving special notice. The most important of these are in the lighting and decoration.

"From the time, now some years since, that the first electric lights in lamps were exhibited outside the Paris Opera House, I have been convinced that electric light, in some form, is the light of the future for use in theatres, not to go further. The peculiar steely blue colour and the flicker, which are inevitable in all systems of 'arc' lights, however, make them unsuitable for use in any but very large buildings. The invention of the 'incandescent lamp' has now paved the way for the application of electricity to lighting houses, and, consequently, theatres.

"The 'arc' light is simply a continuous electric spark, and is nearly the colour of lightning. The incandescent light is produced by heating a filament of carbon to a white heat, and is much the colour of gas - a little clearer. Thanks to an ingenious method of 'shunting' it, the current is easily controllable, and the lights can be raised or lowered at will. The new light is not only used in the audience part of the theatre, but on the stage, for footlights, side and top-lights, &c., and (not of the least importance for the comfort of the performers) in the dressing-rooms - in fact, in every part of the house. This is the first time that it has been attempted to light any public building entirely by electricity. The greatest drawbacks to the enjoyment of theatrical performances are, undoubtedly, the foul air and heat which pervade all theatres. As everyone knows, each gas-burner consumes as much oxygen as many people, and causes great heat besides. The incandescent lamps consume *no* oxygen, and cause no perceptible heat. If the experiment of electric lighting succeeds, there can be no question of the enormous advantages to be gained in purity of air, and coolness - advantages the value of which it is hardly possible to over-estimate.

"The decorations of this theatre are by Messrs. Collinson and Lock.

"I venture to think that, with some few exceptions, the interiors of most theatres hitherto built have been conceived with little, if any, artistic purpose, and generally executed with little completeness, and in a more or less garish manner. Without adopting either of the styles known as 'Queen Anne,' and 'early English' or entering upon the so-called 'Aesthetic' manner, a result has now been produced which I feel sure will be appreciated by all persons of taste. Paintings of cherubim, muses, angels, and mythological deities have been discarded, and the ornament consists entirely of delicate plaster modelling, designed in the manner of the Italian Renaissance. The main colour-tones are white, pale yellow and gold - gold used only for backgrounds, or in large masses, and not - following what may be called, for want of a worse name, the gingerbread school of decorative art - for gilding relief-work or mouldings. The back walls of the boxes and the corridors are in two tones of Venetian red. No painted act-drop is used, but a curtain of creamy satin, quilted, having a fringe at the bottom, and a valance of embroidery of the character of Spanish work, keeps up the consistency of the colour scheme. This curtain is arranged to drape from the centre. The stalls are covered with blue plush of an inky hue, and the balcony seats are of stamped velvet of the same tint, while the curtains of the boxes are of yellowish silk, brocaded with a pattern of decorative flowers in broken colour.

"To turn to a very different subject: I believe a fertile source of annoyance to the public to be the demanding or expecting of fees and gratuities by attendants. This system will, therefore, be discountenanced. Programmes will be furnished, and wraps and umbrellas taken charge of gratuitously.

"The Savoy is, I think, the only theatre in London of which the four outer walls stand open, and in four thoroughfares. There are exits and entrances on all four sides, giving two exits from every part of the house; most valuable conditions with a view to safety from fire; and it is calculated that the entire audience can be cleared out in less than three minutes. The passage and staircases are of fire-resisting materials, and the stage is divided from the front by a solid brick wall, extending from the ground to above the roof. It may be noted that this is the first theatre which has been built under the new Act of 1878, and under the new regulations of the Metropolitan Board of Works, which are especially directed to the prevention of accidents by fire, and are most stringent.

"R. D'Oyly Carte."

In April, 1882, the anniversary of the production of *Patience* was celebrated at the Savoy Theatre by some special ceremonies. Mr. Arthur Sullivan conducted the orchestra; bouquets were presented to the ladies of the audience in all parts of the theatre, and there were new costumes on the stage, and an increased chorus. After the performance members of the audience who were curious regarding the details of the electric lighting of the stage were permitted, on presenting their cards, to pass behind the scenes. A circular issued by the manager gave the following statistical account of the career of this extraordinarily popular opera :-

"During this time the opera has been played under my management 364 times in London, 323 times outside London in Great Britain and Ireland, 180 times in New York, besides 110 times in America outside New York, making a total of 977 times in all. It is calculated that not less than 870,200 persons have paid to see the opera, and the sum of, as nearly as possible, £138,600 has been received for admissions. These figures do not include performances in Australia, of which no return has yet been received, not unauthorized performances in America."

The *caste* of "Patience" was little altered from the first production of the opera in London to its close. Mr. George Grossmith was still the "fleshly poet," Reginald Bunthorne; the graceful idyllic poet, Archibald Grosvenor, being portrayed to the last by Mr. Rutland Barrington, whilst the parts of Patience and of the massive Lady Jane remained in the hands of Miss Leonora Braham and Miss Alice Barnett, who originally created them.

POETS OF THE AESTHETIC SCHOOL

THE principal poets of the school are Dante Gabriel Rossetti, William Michael Rossetti, Thomas Woolner, William Morris, Algernon Charles Swinburne, Arthur O'Shaughnessy, and Oscar Wilde. Robert Browning has some of the characteristics of Aestheticism in his writings, as has also Walt Whitman, the American poet; but neither of these is generally mentioned as of the "Inner Brotherhood." Tennyson's poems, especially "The Idylls," are frequently selected for illustration by Aesthetic artists.

DANTE GABRIEL ROSSETTI

I have already briefly referred to the career of this distinguished man, and the position he took in the early days of the Pre-Raphaelite (or Aesthetic) Movement.

Mr. Dante Gabriel Rossetti was a painter and a poet, about whom during his life much curiosity was felt; he seldom exhibited his paintings, he was not met in public places, and what was known about him appeared mystic, sad, and romantic. Mr. Hall Caine, a friend of the last few years of his life, has recently published his recollections of the poet-painter, and the work is likely to be widely read. It will but intensify the feeling of melancholy engendered by the man and his works, for it shows the waste of power and the loss of genius with which, had they been better disciplined, Rossetti might have fulfilled in maturity the brilliant promise of his youth. In 1870 Rossetti published his first volume of poems, greeted at first with enthusiastic applause, to be followed by a bitter controversy, the poet remained sadly silent for more than ten years, then he published a new volume, the success of which he scarcely lived to see.

Before he came of age Rossetti had done more than any one man of our time to turn Art into a higher road, and in poetry had produced some remarkable, if immature, works full of fire and original genius. But whilst still a comparatively young man, there fell upon him a great domestic misfortune, followed by years of grief and sleeplessness. Living in a large, gloomy house, he courted solitude, and sought to buy sleep in chloral, and the pernicious drug acquired a complete mastery, his ideas became distorted, and he saw, at times none but enemies in those who were his best friends. Under such circumstances the wonder is not that he had of late achieved so little, but that he could produce any real art work at all. Slowly, but surely, his constitution gave way, his friends were powerless to save him, the craving for the drug increased as time went by, until a stroke of paralysis gave an opportunity for the supply of chloral to be cut off. For a brief period his sufferings were great, but when the crisis was over his mind had recovered its equilibrium, and he was no longer troubled by his former hallucinations.

But though now calm in mind, and free from the tormenting craving for the narcotic, the mischief was done, and he gradually faded away into death, which released him on Easter Sunday, the 9th of April, 1882.

His connection with the Pre-Raphaelites, with "The Germ," and his contributions to it have been mentioned; of his paintings less is known, since for some reasons not explained, he seldom exhibited them in public; suffice it to say that they were eagerly sought after, and highly eulogised by connoisseurs whose taste in such matters would usually be accepted as decisive.

Dante Gabriel Rossetti (or more correctly Gabriel Charles Dante Rossetti) was born in Charlotte Street, Portland Place, London, on May 12th, 1828, being the eldest son of Gabriele Rossetti, and brother of William Michael Rossetti, the art critic, and of Maria Francesca and Christina G. Rossetti, both well-known poetesses.

Gabriele Rossetti, the elder, was a native of the Abruzzi, in the kingdom of Naples, and was early distinguished as a patriot and poet, but being implicated in the Neapolitan insurrectionary troubles in 1820-21, he had to leave his position at the Museo Borbonico, fly his native country, and seek refuge in England. He settled in London about 1823, and in 1826 married Frances Polidori, daughter of G. Polidori, formerly secretary to Alfieri, the poet.

Rossetti was appointed Professor of Italian at King's College, and for years his house was the rendezvous of Italian patriots and refugees. He contributed largely to Italian literature, his researches into the life and writings of Dante being regarded as especially valuable, although his speculations on Dante's conceptions gave rise to some considerable controversy. He died in 1854, too early to witness the freedom and unity of his country, for which all his early prospects has been sacrificed. Naturally, young Rossetti's early education was received at King's College, and having from early childhood shown a decided inclination for painting, his parents sensibly fostered and encouraged his genius, so that on leaving King's College, about 1843, he was sent to study first at an art academy near Bedford Square, and afterwards at the Royal Academy Antique School, never, however, going to the Life School of the Royal Academy; and the deficiencies of this early training were apparent throughout his career as an artist, especially as regards draughtsmanship.

He left the Royal Academy in 1849, and in the same year he exhibited his picture of the *Girlhood of Mary Virgin*. In 1846 Mr. Ford Madox Brown exhibited designs in the Westminster Competition, and young Rossetti was so deeply impressed with the cartoons, that he wrote asking to be permitted to become a pupil of Mr. Brown, who himself was but a few years the senior of Rossetti.

Although Rossetti did not long continue to work in Mr. Brown's studio, the two became life-long friends, and Rossetti always acknowledged that he owed much in art to the influences of Mr. Brown, whose archaeological tastes harmonised well with his own; but whilst Rossetti early joined enthusiastically in the so-called Pre-Raphaelite Movement, Mr. Madox Brown did not, for the reason that he disapproved of cliques and coteries in art. Indeed all the artists soon departed from the principles of exact realism (the "holy awkwardness") they had laid down for their guidance, with the exception, perhaps, of Mr. Holman Hunt.

The recent burning of the Exhibition Palace in Sydney has probably deprived the world of a picture which might be described as one of the treasures of modern English art. Mr. Ford Madox Brown's celebrated picture of "Chaucer reading his Poems at the Court of Edward III" was lately bought for the National Museum of Sydney, and was on exhibition in the building which has been destroyed. It was one of Mr. Madox Brown's earliest works, and was perhaps the first great embodiment of the artistic principle which was afterwards called Pre-Raphaelitism. While the painter was working at it, his studio was entered for the first time by Dante Rossetti. Mr. Rossetti had previously written to Mr. Brown, asking to be allowed to become his pupil, because of the admiration he felt for some of Mr. Madox Brown's still earlier paintings. Rossetti came in good time, for Mr. Brown not merely accepted him as a pupil, but made his face the model for that of the principal figure in the picture. The head of the Chaucer is believed to be the only really good portrait of Dante Gabriel Rossetti that was ever taken. It is much to be regretted that such a painting should not have been preserved in some English Gallery. Apart altogether from its striking merits as a work of art, it had distinct historical value for the English student as the precursor of a school which has undoubtedly made a deep mark on its time.

Rossetti's "The Girlhood of Mary Virgin" was exhibited at the Portland Gallery, an exhibition in rivalry to the Royal Academy, which existed but a very short time. He did not again exhibit in public until about 1856, when he and his friends opened a small collection of their own works at 4, Russel-place, Fitzroy-square. The principal contributors to this interesting collection were Millais, Holman Hunt, Madox Brown, J. D. Watson, and W. B. Scott.

In 1857, whilst engaged on the Union frescoes, Rossetti became acquainted with Burne-Jones, Swinburne, and William Morris, all, at that time, Oxford undergraduates. E. Burne-Jones was intended for a clerical career, but, mainly at the instigation of Rossetti, he abandoned that profession to become a painter, and by his works to add lustre and distinction to the movement initiated by Rossetti. Some years later Mr. E. B. Jones and Rossetti, Madox Brown, and a few others, associated with William Morris in establishing the now well-known art firm of Morris and Co., remaining partners in that enterprise until about

1874, when a dissolution took place, leaving the business in the hands of the gentleman whose name it bore, and whose abilities had made it a success.

With an hereditary love for Dante, some of Rossetti's best work as an artist derived its inspiration from the "Vita Nuova," but in the usual acceptance of the word, his paintings could never be popular. Mystical representations of unfamiliar poetry, and weird, out-of-the-way legends will interest only a few romantic persons who are initiated into the strange symbolism of such art.

A. C. Swinburne, in his notes on the Academy pictures in 1868, said :- "The present year has other pictures to be proud of, not submitted to the loose and slippery judgements of an Academy," and after describing one by Whistler, he adds :-

"It is well known that the painter of whom I now propose to speak has never suffered exclusion or acceptance at the hands of any Academy. It is not less well known that his work must always hold its place as second in significance and value to no work done by any English painter of his time. Among the many great works of Mr. D. G. Rossetti, I know of none greater that his two latest. These are types of sensual beauty and spiritual, the siren and the sibyl, 'Lady Lilith,' and 'Sibylla Palmifera.' "

These, and several other paintings he enumerates, were afterwards set to music, so to speak, in poems written by D. G. Rossetti.

One of the models who sat to him was Miss Elizabeth Eleanor Siddal, a young lady of singular personal beauty, with a natural genius for painting, and a cultivated taste for poetry. Before long the lady became as much a pupil as a model, kindred tastes led to friendship and to love, and in 1860 they were married, but their happiness was of short duration.

It has been noticed as a strange and painful coincidence that both Dante Gabriel Rossetti and his wife died prematurely from the effects of opiates.

After the birth of a still-born child, Mrs. Rossetti fell into ill-health and suffered acutely from neuralgia. To soothe the pain and get sleep, she would take some preparation of opium - chloral was not then the fashionable drug it has since become. One evening, Mr. Rossetti, returning from some engagement, was glad to find that his wife had retired for the night and was asleep. He moved quietly about the room, so as not to disturb her. After a while, he grew troubled at the stillness of her sleep, and, bending over her he spoke to her. His voice did not rouse her; and he discovered that she was insensible. A doctor, called in in a hurry, applied all possible remedies. It was too late. Mrs. Rossetti never recovered consciousness; she had taken an overdose of opium, and died of its effects. This was in 1862, after two years only of married life.

The poet-painter felt bitterly the death of one whose beauty inspired some of his most notable works (as, for instance, the woodcut illustrations to Tennyson's poems), and whose artistic gifts made her a sympathetic helpmate. He fell for a while into a state of profound melancholy, and refusing to be known as a poet, when he could not share his fame with her, he buried in her coffin the MS. of his as yet unpublished poems.

When quite a young man, it is true, he had contributed several short poems of great promise to *The Germ*, and in 1861, he published a work entitled "The Early Italian Poets," which contained a translation of Dante's *Vita Nuova*; this was republished in 1874 with some alterations under the title of

"Dante and his Circle."

There is also in the library of the British Museum a curious little work, entitled -

SIR HUGH THE HERON

A Legendary Tale in Four Parts, by Gabriel Rossetti, Jun.

> "Sir Hugh the Heron bold,
> Baron of Twisell, and of Ford,
> And Captain of the Hold."
>
> Scott's *Marmion*, Canto 1.

This bears the imprint, "London, 1843. G. Polidori's Private Press, 15, Park Village East, Regent's Park. For private circulation." At that time young Rossetti amused himself with attempts at poetry, and his grandfather Polidori, who had set up an amateur printing press in his own house printed off some copies of the poem in question, having a much higher opinion of it than the author had in after years, when he was somewhat annoyed to find that a few copies were actually in circulation and eagerly sought after by collectors of literary curiosities.

More than seven years after the death of his wife, when time had somewhat soothed his sorrow, and lessened his deep sense of bereavement, he was prevailed upon by the entreaties of his friends to recover the lost poems. After some preliminary trouble he obtained the consent of the Home Secretary to have the grave in Highgate Cemetery opened. The manuscript was found in the coffin but little injured, and very shortly afterwards his first volume, simply entitled "Poems," was published, and at once came into favour, seven editions being issued in rapid succession, a result which must in part, no doubt, be attributed to popular curiosity with regard to the author, and the connection he was known to have with the Pre-Raphaelite School. In many of the high-class Reviews, the poems were at first enthusiastically received, but it was not long before they were brought before the public in a manner perhaps more prominent than pleasant, owing to the virulent attacks made upon them by a certain class of critics, whose fastidious prudery led them to republish extracts from his works with a lewd suggestiveness of purpose never intended by the author. His second volume, "Ballads and Sonnets," was published by Ellis and White in 1881.

He had lived for some years past in comparative seclusion, and owing to this and a certain strangeness of manner, an impression had gone abroad that his intellect was affected. This, however, was not the case, but Mr. Rossetti had, for a long period, suffered from habitual sleeplessness - a terrible affliction which often visits men whose brain power has been severely taxed - and the remedy he tried, namely chloral, whilst it gave him some sort of temporary relief, was, in the long run, far worse than the original evil.

He died quietly and calmly on Easter Sunday last, at Birchington, near Margate, retaining his intellect to the last. Though his father was an Italian, and his mother of Italian extraction, it is said that D. G. Rossetti never visited that country, yet his works are suffused with the sunny glow of the southern clime, and instinct with the life and fire of Roman art. In the foremost rank of our modern painters, and as a poet unequalled in a certain *genre* of his own (for some of his sonnets are near perfection), the world of art and letters will long lament the loss of Rossetti.

He was followed to his grave in the quiet little churchyard of Birchington by his mother, his sister Miss Christina Rossetti, the poetess, his brother Mr. William Michael Rossetti, and a number of literary and artistic friends; Mr. E. Burne-Jones, who was to have attended, was taken so ill on his way to the ceremony that he was obliged to return home.

A writer in the *Standard* recently summed up his career in an appreciative notice, from which I take the following :-

"It was not till 1870 that he sanctioned the appearance in a volume of the compositions which had for a long while been the delight of his friends. He delayed a similar reserve in the exercise of his art as painter. With the single exception, we believe, of his picture of "Dante's Dream," purchased by the Liverpool Picture Gallery, none of his canvases were exhibited to the common eye. He sold them by private arrangement to his acquaintances, and he had singularly few, if any, transactions with dealers. Yet, though the field of display which he allowed himself was so severely limited, the area of his influence was large. There is a sense in which he might be called a born leader of men. He was full of an enthusiasm that speedily communicated itself to those around him. He had great conversational and even oratorial gifts. His voice was full and sweet, and his manner, when he chose, exceedingly attractive. Whatever effeminacy some critics might detect in his poetry or his pictures, his presence was robust, manly, and, in many respects, typically English. There has, perhaps, never been such an instance of a man qualified to win a really high place in contemporary Art and Letters who so persistently, as far as the outer world was concerned, concealed his light under a bushel. As a poet, Rossetti is, and from the first day that he began to write was, essentially picturesque. As a painter, he began by being singularly unpicturesque. The frescoes with which he decorated the Oxford Union are a marked advance in this direction upon any of his previous works; they are also, perhaps, the best-known specimens of his artistic skill. The designs may be charged with a mystical meaning of their own, which only the esoteric worshippers of the artist can fully appreciate. But they possess, also, indisputably that attribute of picturesqueness which was partially absent from his earlier efforts. It is no exaggeration to say that their completion was an event both in Modern Letters and Art. They probably impressed the imagination of Mr. William Morris and Mr. Burne-Jones - then undergraduates at Oxford; they lent not a little assistance to that school of poetic thought which may be best associated with the name of Mr. Swinburne."

Mr. G. A. Sala (who has always a kindly word to say, and an eloquent way of saying it, about his brother *littérateurs*,) had known him for nearly thirty years, and speaks of him as intellectually one of the most gifted of men; personally gentle, amiable, truthful and upright.

Soon after his death it was announced that his brother was about to organise a large exhibition of his works, and other papers stated that the Fine Art Society proposed to hold an exhibition of his paintings soon, at their gallery in New Bond Street.

It is difficult to reconcile these statements with the following intimation given in the *Academy* :-

"We are authorized to state that the family and friends of the late Dante Rossetti are concerned and grieved at what they cannot but think the inconsiderate haste which has been displayed in certain quarters to announce forthcoming exhibitions of the painter's works. They desire it to be known, first, that all pictures painted by Rossetti, except one belonging to the City of Liverpool, were sold under copyright restrictions which cover control of exhibition; next, that the holders of the important works privately decline to lend their pictures, except to the executor of his estate; and, last, that they cannot countenance the exhibition of the lesser works to the exclusion of the greater ones, on which Rossetti's fame must finally rest. They appeal to owners everywhere to help them (and prevent complications), by withholding from all applicants promises of loan at the present stage."

Naturally the sale of Mr. Rossetti's effects attracted a large number of persons to the gloomy old-fashioned residence in Cheyne Walk, Chelsea, and many of the articles sold went for prices very far in excess of their intrinsic value, the total sum realised being over £3,000.

The competition for some of the books was very keen, especially for the presentation copies; one of these was Swinburne's "Atalanta in Calydon;" inscribed, *Dante Gabriel Rossetti, from his affectionate A. C. Swinburne*, being a first copy printed off before the dedication was in type. This little volume (a copy of which can be obtained from the publisher for six shillings), speedily ran up to eight and a half guineas; there being then a dispute, as two bidders claimed it, the auctioneer put it up again, and it was finally sold for thirty-one guineas.

Our old friend, *The Germ*, the four parts in wrappers as originally published at one shilling each part, sold for six guineas; and an original MS. and sketch-book of William Blake was bought by Mr. Murray for 105 guineas, the price in this instance being in proportion to the value of the volume, which contains a number of new poems and sketches by Blake, and is, of course, unique.

This curious little volume had been purchased for ten shillings by Rossetti, in 1849, from Mr. Palmer, an attendant in the British Museum, and was of undoubted authenticity. For many years it was a source of pleasure and profit to its possessor, and furnished many interesting details to Gilchrist's "Life and

Works of Blake," to which work, indeed, both the Rossettis rendered valuable literary assistance, as was gratefully acknowledged by Mrs. Gilchrist, her husband having died before the new edition of the work was ready for the press.

But during the sale of these books on that fine July afternoon, in the dingy studio hung round with the lovely but melancholy faces of Proserpine and Pandora, despite the noise and the throng and the witticisms of the auctioneer, a sad feeling of desecration must have crept over many of those who were present at the dispersion of the household goods and favourite books of that man who hated the vulgar crowd. Gazing through the open windows they could see the tall trees waving their heads in a sorrowful sort of way in the summer breeze, throwing their shifting shadows over the neglected grass-grown paths, once the haunt of the stately peacocks whose mediaeval beauty had such a strange fascination for Rossetti, and whose feathers are now the accepted favours of his apostles and admirers.

And so their gaze would wander back again to that mysterious face upon the wall, that face some say the grandest of the world, a lovely one in truth, with its wistful, woful, passionate eyes, its masses of heavy wavy auburn hair, its sweet sad mouth with the full ripe lips; a face that seemed to say the sad old lines:

" 'Tis better to have loved and lost,
Than never to have loved at all."

And then would come the monotonous cry of the auctioneer
GOING! GOING! GONE!
to disturb the *reverie*, and to call one back to this matter-of-fact world which Dante Gabriel Rossetti, painter and poet, has left.

———————

BUCHANAN'S ATTACK ON ROSSETTI

On the publication of Rossetti's "Poems" in 1870, their originality and power at once claimed general attention, and, as a natural consequence, the envy and detraction of rival poets, and the enemies of the school with which his name and fame were identified.

Amongst these critics was Robert Buchanan, who, as "Caliban," had already attacked Swinburne in the verses entitled, *The Session of the Poets.* In that poem, it will be remembered, that Buchanan mentioned himself as taking part in a solemn meeting of the leading poets of the day, although at that period (1866) he was little known, and would most certainly not have been included in such a select company by any other writer.

However this may be, an article appeared in the *Contemporary Review* of October, 1871, entitled, "The Fleshly School of Poetry," being a fierce attack on the Poems of Dante G. Rossetti, which were then already in the fifth edition; this article was signed *"Thomas Maitland."*

It being a distinctive feature of that Review that all articles should bear the actual signatures of their authors, some speculation took place as to this unknown *"Thomas Maitland,"* whose virulent article appeared amongst others all bearing well-known names.

It was at once set down as an assumed name, and for two reasons was assigned to Robert Buchanan; first, because it was known that on every possible occasion he attacked the school to which he assigned the works of Rossetti, and secondly, because in the opening passage of the article where he disputes Rossetti's right to be considered as anything but a minor poet, he inserted his own name amongst the first poets of the day.

The article commences thus :-

"Suppose that on the occasion of any performance of Hamlet the actors who perform the parts of Rosencrantz and Guildenstern, were by means of what is technically known as 'gagging,' to make themselves just as prominent as the leading character, the result would be, to say the least of it, astonishing; yet a very similar effect is produced on the unprejudiced mind when the 'walking gentlemen' of the Fleshly School of poetry, who bear precisely the same relation to Mr. Tennyson, as Rosencrantz and Guildenstern do to the Prince of Denmark in the play, obtrude their lesser identities, and parade their smaller idiosyncrasies in the front rank of leading performers. In their own place the gentlemen are interesting and useful.

"Pursuing still further the theatrical analogy, the present drama of poetry might be cast as follows :-

"Hamlet by Mr. Alfred Tennyson; Horatio, Mr. Matthew Arnold; Voltimand, Mr. Bailey; Cornelius, Mr. R. Buchanan; Rosencrantz, Mr. Swinburne; Guildenstern, Mr. W. Morris; Osric, Mr. D. G. Rossetti; A Gentleman, Mr. Robert Lytton.

"It will be seen that we have left no place for Mr. Browning, who may be said, however, to play the leading character in his own peculiar fashion on alternate nights."

It was this paragraph which betrayed the author of the article, for assuredly no one but Robert Williams Buchanan would have inserted the name of Buchanan amongst, and as one of, the leading poets; and, as the *Athenaeum* remarked, when Mr. Buchanan accused Rossetti of copying him, and classed himself above him as a poet, and along with Mr. Matthew Arnold, he was really singing his own praises over an assumed name.

On Dec. 2nd, 1871, the *Athenaeum* said :-

"Mr. Sidney Colvin is, we believe, preparing to answer in the pages of the *Contemporary Review*, an article which lately appeared in that magazine entitled 'The Fleshly School of Poetry,' by Thomas Maitland, a *nom de plume* assumed by Mr. Robert Buchanan."

But the following week Mr. S. Colvin wrote to say that it was not his intention to attack the article in question, but that he would remain contented with having pointed out that in a magazine adopting the rule of signature to its articles, one had been admitted in which the author gratified his personal spite by attacking various other authors, delivering his cowardly thrust from behind the shield of an imaginary "Thomas Maitland."

In the same paper appeared the following singular letter from Messrs. Strahan & Co., the publishers of the *Contemporary* :-

"In your last issue you associate the name of Mr. Robert Buchanan with the article, 'The Fleshly School of Poetry,' by Thomas Maitland. You might with equal propriety associate with the article the name of Mr. Robert Browning, or Mr. Robert Lytton, or any other Robert."

But just below this very equivocal communication, was one from Mr. Buchanan, saying :-

"I certainly wrote the article on 'The Fleshly School of Poetry,' but I had nothing to do with the signature. Mr. Strahan can corroborate me thus far, as he is best aware of the inadvertence which led to the suppression of my own name. Permit me to say further, that although I should have preferred not to resuscitate so slight a thing, I have now requested Mr. Strahan to republish the criticism, with many additions but no material alterations, and with my name on the title page."

To which the editor of the *Athenaeum* appended this note :-

"Mr. Buchanan's letter is an edifying commentary on Messrs. Strahan's. Messrs. Strahan apparently think it is a matter of no importance whether signatures are correct or not, and that Mr. Browning had as much to do with the article as Mr. Buchanan. Mr. Buchanan seems equally indifferent, but he now claims the critique as his. It is a pity the publishers of the *Contemporary Review* should be in such uncertainty about the authorship of articles in that magazine. It may be only a matter of taste, but we prefer, if we are reading an article written by Mr. Buchanan, that it should be signed by him, especially when he praises his own poems; and that little 'inadvertencies' of this kind should not be left uncorrected till the public find them out."

Dante Gabriel Rossetti, in the same number, wrote a crushing reply to Buchanan's article, which he styles *The Stealthy School of Criticism*. He refers to the unfair nature of Mr. Buchanan's attacks upon his poetry, and shows that by extracts taken apart from their contexts, his meanings were distorted and his ideas misrepresented; and that, in fact, Mr. Buchanan had, by hi selections and suggestions, rendered impure that which was chaste, and even imported indecency where none was originally to be found.

He adds :-

"It would be humiliating, need one come to serious detail, to have to refute such an accusation as that of 'binding oneself by solemn league and pictorial art.' Indeed, what I have said already is substantially enough to refute it, even did I not feel sure that a fair balance of my poetry must, of itself, do so in the eyes of every candid reader. I say nothing of my pictures; but those who know them will laugh at the idea.

"That I may, nevertheless, take a wider view than some poets or critics, of how much, in the material conditions absolutely given to man to deal with as distinct from his spiritual aspirations, is admissible within the limits of art - this, I say, is possible enough; nor do I wish to shrink from such responsibility. But to state that I do so to the ignoring or over-shadowing of spiritual beauty, is an absolute falsehood, impossible to be put forward except in the indulgence of prejudice and rancour."

Notwithstanding the reproofs he had met with from the contemporary press, Mr. Buchanan persisted in reprinting his article, which was published in 1872 by Strahan & Co., in a pamphlet of ninety-seven pages, having been greatly enlarged by the addition of chapters violently attacking Swinburne and Beaudelaire, the French poet, from whose *Fleurs du Mal*, he accuses Swinburne of stealing many of his ideas, as he had previously accused Rossetti of stealing from himself! - Of course he also accuses Swinburne of fleshliness, and of even surpassing Beaudelaire in the sensualism of his art.

After a time the pamphlet was suppressed (one may say it ought never to have been published), and is now very difficult to meet with.

In justice to Mr. Buchanan, it must be stated that he afterwards made handsome amends, admitting that he had been unjust to Rossetti, as a poet, and explaining that much of his criticism had also been unfairly construed, and misapplied.

WILLIAM MICHAEL ROSSETTI

Born in 1829, he edited *The Germ* in 1850, and in 1867

published a volume entitled "Fine Art, Chiefly Contemporary," and in 1878, "Lives of Famous Poets," (inscribed to two beloved memories, Oliver Madox Brown, writer and painter, died 5th November, 1874, aged 19. Maria Francesca Rossetti, writer and sister of the poor, died 24th Nov., 1876, aged 49); besides editing the works of Keats, Shelley, and numerous other poets included in "Moxon's Popular Series," to each of which he prefixed critical memoirs.

To him it was that Swinburne dedicated his magnificent work on William Blake, and the terms in which he addresses Rossetti breathe affection and respect, such as, indeed, appears generally to exist amongst this curious circle of gifted men.

He thus concludes the dedication :-

"Friendship needs no cement of reciprocal praise; and this book dedicated to you from the first, and owing to your guidance as much as to my goodwill, whatever it may have of worth, wants no extraneous allusion to explain why it should rather be inscribed with your name than with another. Nevertheless, I will say that now of all times it gives me pleasure to offer you such a token of friendship as I have at hand to give. I can but bring you brass for the gold you send me; but between equals and friends there can be no question of barter. Like Diomed, I take what I am given and offer what I have. Such as it is, I know you will accept it with more allowance than it deserves; but one thing you will not over-rate - the affectionate admiration, the grateful remembrance, which needs no public expression on the part of your friend,

"A. C. Swinburne."

"November, 1866."

The volume entitled "Fine Art, Chiefly Contemporary"

(published by Macmillan in 1867), consisted principally of art criticisms, which had previously appeared in various magazines and reviews. Amongst them was a short paper on *Pre-Raphaelitism*, reproduced from the *Spectator*, in which it had originally appeared as far back as 1851. He thus described the object the P. R. B. had in view :-

"The painters before Raphael had worked in often more than partial ignorance of the positive rules of art, and unaffected by conventional rules. These were not known of in their days; and they neither invented nor discovered them. It is to the latter fact, and not the former, that the adoption of the name "Pre-Raphaelites" by the artists in question is to be ascribed. Pre-Raphaelites truly they are - but of the nineteenth century. Their aim is the same - truth; and their process the same - exactitude of study from Nature; but their practice is different, for their means are enlarged."

In addition to his labours as an Art and Poetical critic, Mr. W. M. Rossetti holds an appointment in the Civil Service, nor must it be forgotten that he, too, is a poet, as the following exquisite sonnet will show :-

"SHELLEY'S HEART.
"*To* Edward John Trelawny.

" 'What has surprised us all was that the heart remained entire. In snatching this relic away from the fiery furnace, my hand was severely burnt.' - Trelawny's *Recollections of Shelley*.

"Trelawny's hand, which held'st the sacred heart,
    The heart of Shelley, and hast felt the fire
    Wherein the drossier frame-work of that lyre
Of heaven and earth was molten - but its part

Immortal echoes always, and shall dart
    Pangs to keen love to human souls, and dire
    Ecstatic sorrow of joy, as higher and higher
They mount to know thee, Shelley, what thou art.
Trelawny's hand, did then the outward burn
    As once the inward? O cor cordium,
    Which *wast* a spirit of love, and now a clot,
    What other other flame was wont to come
Lambent from thee to fainter hearts, and turn -
    Red like thy death-pyre's heat, their lukewarmth hot!
                  "Wm. M. Rossetti, 1871."

THOMAS WOOLNER

The first poem printed in *The Germ* of January, 1850, was one by Thomas Woolner, a sculptor by profession, and an original member of the P. R. B. This poem, entitled "My Beautiful Lady," was reprinted, with additions, by Macmillan and Co. in 1863, and has run to several editions. It is an exquisite tale of love and sorrow, full of tender sentiment and bright description.

It thus portrays the lady of his love, in lines which recall some of Sir John Suckling's sweetest fancies :-

"I love my lady; she is very fair;
Her brow is wan, and bound by simple hair:
    Her spirit sits aloof, and high,
    But glances from her tender eye
    In sweetness droopingly.

"Her warbling voice, though ever low and mild,
Oft makes me feel as strong wine would a child:

And though her hand be airy light
Of touch, it moves me with its might,
    As would a sudden fright.

"My Lady walks as I have watched a swan
Swim where a glory on the water shone:
    There, ends of willow branches ride,
    Quivering in the flowing tide,
    By the deep river's side.

"Fresh beauties, howsoe'er she moves, are stirred:
    As the sunned bosom of a humming bird
    At each pant lifts some fiery hue,
    Fierce gold, bewildering green or blue;
    The same, yet ever new.

"What time she walks beneath the flowering May,
Quite sure am I the scented blossoms say,
    'O Lady with the sunlit hair!
    Stay and drink our odorous air,
    The incense that we bear.

"Thy beauty, Lady, we would ever shade;
For near to thee, our sweetness might not fade.'
    And could the trees be broken-hearted
    The green sap surely must have smarted,
    When my Lady parted.

"How beautiful she is! a glorious gem
She shines above the summer diadem
    Of flowers! And when her light is seen
    Among them, all in reverence lean
    To her, their tending Queen."

Mr. Woolner has recently published another poem on the

pretty old mythological legend of Pygmalion, which must always have a special interest to sculptors.

It is not often that one is gratified with such a fitness of things as that a sculptor, eminent and enthusiastic in his art, should be a poet also, and should choose the antique legend of "Pygmalion" for his theme. In "Pygmalion" the verse has often a certain chiselled severity of outline and an almost sculpturesque solidity of form. Nor is it wanting in antique simplicity, and a power of presenting images of grace and beauty without overstepping the limits of the art which finds expression in words. Yet, here and there, Mr. Woolner, more or less unconsciously, betrays a spirit and a bitterness of more modern temper when he glances at the besetting trials and troubles of the artist's life and vocation, of which, indeed, he has had a fair share.

WILLIAM MORRIS

William Morris, born in 1834, is by profession a designer of art decorations, wall-papers, carpets, and such-like ornamental household necessaries, in which kind of business the new styles inaugurated and encouraged by the Aesthetes have created quite a revolution. He has recently published a volume of lectures on the decorative arts, in which the influence of Ruskin's teaching is strongly shown. He insists on the necessity of good, sound, honest work, both in art and in trade, before all flimsy meretricious show and finery; he also advocates the opening of our art collections and museums to the public every day in the week; and the more general training of the people in the rudiments of artistic work.

In the weary warfare against ignorance and bigotry, the position taken up by men like Morris, who have a wide influence over the rising generation, is especially noteworthy in connection with the Sunday Question. It is almost hopeless to look for any general improvement in the art tastes of the *people* so long as the art collections are closed on the only day of the week when the *people* could visit them. In the summer, when people can, and do, seek Nature's God in Nature's Glories, the loss is less felt than in the long, damp, dreary days of winter, when to walk the streets is muddy misery, only a trifle less gloomy than to remain in the small close rooms of the dark dingy houses our poorer classes are compelled to inhabit.

Homes indeed so dismal and desolate, that the public house near by, with its glare of gas and its poisonous gin, tempts poor men to their ruin; whilst others, more sober, but scarcely less miserable, brood over the iniquitous system which places nearly all the cumulative value of land and houses in the hands of a few hereditary landowners, and compels the industrious poor to inhabit hovels which would be deemed unfit for my lord's hunters, or his hounds.

Many leaders of thought in the present day are, theoretically at least, Republicans; whether Mr. Morris holds such opinions I can not say, but one thing is clear, that those who would wish to spread revolutionary doctrines, have but to leave things as they are for a few years longer, in order to see such a terrible upheaval against our territorial system of hereditary and entailed estates, as the world has not witnessed since the French Revolution. Our poor cannot live where they choose, but must live near their work, every shilling that can be ground out of them for rent is mercilessly exacted, whilst the value of the land is constantly increasing, to the benefit of such as can claim descent from the robbers of Henry the Eighth's glorious reign, from the mistresses of the virtuous Charles the Second, or the favourites of George the Fourth of pious memory. For of such is the kingdoms of an hereditary, irresponsible, legislative aristocracy, which originally obtained its grants of the land on certain conditions, all of which are systematically evaded.

Like Ruskin, Morris decries the fevered strain for money, and is at times somewhat severe on the modern appliances of steam and machinery as being detrimental to the beauties f nature; and, indeed, he would fain

"Forget six counties overhung with smoke

Forget the snorting steam and piston stroke."

As a poet, his fame rests chiefly upon a long and beautiful work entitled "The Earthly Paradise," a poem in four parts, named Spring, Summer, Autumn, and Winter. These volumes contain twenty-five tales in verse, viz. :- The Wanderers; Atalanta's Race; The Man born to be King; The Doom of King Acrisius; The Proud King; Cupid and Psyche; The Writing on the Image; The Love of Alcestis; The Lady of the Land; The Son of Croesus; The Watching of the Falcon; Pygmalion and the Image; Ogier, the Dane; The Death of Paris; The Land East of the Sun and West of the Moon; Acontius and Cydippe; The Man who never laughed again; The Story of Rhodope; The Lovers of Gudrun; The Golden Apples; The Fostering of Aslaug; Bellerophon at Argos; The Ring given to Venus; Bellerophon in Lycia; The Hill of Venus.

His other published poems and translations are :- "The Life and Death of Jason," a poem, in seventeen books; "Love is Enough; or The Freeing of Pharamond," a morality; "The

Defence of Guenevere," and other poems; "The Story of Sigurd and Volsung, and the Fall of the Niblungs"; "The Story of Grettir the Strong," translated from the Icelandic of the Grettis Saga (one of the most remarkable prose works of ancient Icelandic literature); "The Story of the Volsungs and Niblungs," with songs translated from the Elder Edda; "Three Northern Love Stories," and other tales translated from the Icelandic, in these translations Mr. Morris was assisted by Mr. F. Magnusson.

In this year's Grosvenor Gallery a very fine portrait of William Morris was exhibited by W. B. Richmond, showing a handsome genial face and massive intellectual head - the poet to the life.

So far, then, the Aesthetic union between painting, sculpture, the decorative arts, and poetry, has been amply exemplified; we next come to a distinguished poet, who is, however, purely and simply, a man of letters, namely A. C. Swinburne.

ALGERNON CHARLES SWINBURNE

There are probably few literary men who would hesitate for a moment in assigning to Swinburne the title of King of the Aesthetic poets, and in 1860, long before the movement became fashionable, he had dedicated his tragic drama, "The Queen Mother," to Dante Gabriel Rossetti, and his "Laus Veneris" to E. Burne-Jones, to which artist the place of honour is now assigned in the Grosvenor Gallery. One of Burne-Jones's most famous pictures also has the title, "Laus Veneris." In the same volume of poems there was also a sonnet to the eccentric artist, J. M. Whistler.

Algernon Charles Swinburne (an Oxford man) is undoubtedly a poet of great power, an excellent scholar and linguist, and one of the most accomplished men of letters of the day; masterly as a critic, he is unsurpassed in the vigour and elegance of his prose writings.

Many of those who know him only as a Poet of strongly Republican tendencies would be surprised to hear of his aristocratic descent, and probably Swinburne, like Prior, would rest content with those ancestors common to us all. His grandfather, Sir John Swinburne, held a baronetcy which dated as far back as 1660, belonging to a family, which, through good and evil fortune, had adhered to the Stuart Dynasty. Sir John lived to the age of 98 (he died in 1860), and during his long life he enjoyed the friendship of most of the leading literary and poetical celebrities both in France and England, connecting one century with another, as he could also one country with another, and remembering as clearly Mirabeau and John Wilkes, as he did Turner and Mulready. The poet's father (a younger son of Sir John) held a commission in the Royal Navy, and in 1836 he married Lady Jane Henrietta, daughter of the Earl of Ashburnham, so that Algernon Charles Swinburne is descended from two of our oldest aristocratic families.

Though of equally noble birth with Shelley, Byron, Alfieri, Victor Hugo, or Henri Rochefort, and possessing quite as keen an interest in the progress of democracy as they, he refused a seat in Parliament when one was offered to him by the Reform League, preferring to devote his life and energies to literature - and perhaps the choice was a wise one, for the position of a Radical Member in our English Parliament is not, as yet, an enviable one.

He passed five years at Eton, and nearly four at Oxford;

since then his pen has been most prolific, producing twenty volumes at least of prose and verse, besides almost innumerable articles and reviews; the splendour of his genius as a poet and critic is now generally admitted, but his best friends must regret that the ardent enthusiasm of his nature will not permit him to husband his resources, and so avoid the chronic nervousness and physical weakness which so often disable those who overtax their brain power.

Born in 1837, he is still a young man, yet his name has been prominently before the public for a good many years, and his works are numerous and varied in character, as will be seen from the following list :- "The Queen Mother and Rosamond," 1860; "Atalanta in Calydon," 1865; "Chastelard, a Tragedy," 1865; "Poems and Ballads," 1866; "Notes on Poems and Reviews," 1866; "Songs of Italy," 1867; "Essay on William Blake," 1868; "Notes on the Royal Academy Exhibition," 1868; "Siena," 1868; "Ode on the French Republic," 1870; "Songs before Sunrise," 1871; "Under the Microscope," 1872; "Tombeau de Théophile Gautier" (containing poems by Swinburne in English, French, Latin, and Greek; Paris, 1873); "Bothwell, a Tragedy," 1874; "Essays and Studies," 1875; "Songs of Two Nations," 1875; "Essay on George Chapman," 1875; "Note on the Muscovite Crusade," 1876; "Erechtheus, a Tragedy," 1876; "Note on Charlotte Brontë," 1877; "Poems and Ballads," second series, 1878; "A Study of Shakespeare," 1880;[5] "Songs of the Springtides," 1880: "Studies in Song," 1880; "Mary Stuart," and various other poems.

---

[5] Thus dedicated to the greatest living authority on Shakespeare, the learned and genial James Orchard Halliwell Phillipps. - "That a sample of excerpt given from this book, while as yet, save in design, unfinished, should have found such favour in your sight, and won such approval at your hands as you then by word alike and action, so

cordially expressed, is reason enough why I should inscribe it with your name: even if I felt less pleasure in the reflection and the record, that this little labour of a life-long love had at once the doubly good fortune and the doubly grateful success, to be praised by those who have earned the praise and thanks of all true Shakespearian scholars, and dispraised by such as have deserved their natural doom to reap neither, but from the harvest of their own applause or that of their fellows. It might be hard for a personally unbiassed judgement to strike the balance of genuine value and significance between these two forms of acknowledgement, but it will be evident which is to me the more precious, when I write your name above my own on the votive scroll, which attaches my offering to the shrine of Shakespeare. - Algernon Charles Swinburne."

Thus, although he has made his name as one of the first of England's poets, his contributions to prose literature are also of great importance; as a critic he is unrivalled for keenness of insight and the power and brilliance of his language. He, at least, is a living exemplification of Ch. Baudelaire's axiom :-

"Tous les grands poëtes deviennent naturellement, fatalement, critiques. Il serait prodigieux qu'un critique devint poëte, mais il est impossible qu'un poëte ne contienne pas un critique."

There can be little doubt but that the part of Reginald Bunthorne, the Fleshly Poet in Gilbert's opera, was a mild satire upon Swinburne, upon whom the title of a fleshly poet was conferred some years since by Robert Buchanan, the critic, in his fierce little book called "The Fleshly School." Besides which, Mr. George Grossmith's make-up for the part added some slight personal resemblance to the literary skits contained in the piece.

Now, the rival poet, excellently portrayed by that fascinating actor, Mr. Rutland Barrington, was as undoubtedly intended for Mr. Oscar Wilde. Archibald Grosvenor, the idyllic poet, appeared as a tall, handsome young man in the style of dress affected by Mr. Oscar Wilde, and there were numerous allusions throughout the piece both to his personal good looks, and to his mildly idyllic poetry, such, for instance, as in the decalet, "Gentle Jane."

It will be remarked that Swinburne's first volume was published when he was but twenty-three years of age, and, as is usual with English reviewers, the work of the young poet was at once marked out for slaughter. In every other profession the first efforts of a young beginner are treated with a little indulgence, and are more leniently criticised than the labours of an experienced and veteran performer. It is otherwise with the young singing bird: let him but once raise his head to sing, when down swoop upon him the vultures of the Press, and if they cannot peck the life out of him, they so screech round him, and buffet about him with their wings, that the noise they make, though it has no music in it, effectually drowns his voice. Chatterton was killed in this manner, and so was Keats; Byron had too much stamina for them. He turned fiercely upon them, in "English Bards and Scotch Reviewers," and beat them so soundly that the laugh was all on his side.

Old Professor Wilson (Christopher North) in *Blackwood's Magazine*, attempted to extinguish Alfred Tennyson in the same manner, but the future Poet Laureate contemptuously replied in the following lines -

"You did late review my lays,
Crusty Christopher,
You did mingle blame and praise,
Rusty Christopher.
When I learnt from whom it came,

> I forgave you all the blame,
>
> Musty Christopher;
>
> I could *not* forgive the praise,
>
> Fusty Christopher.

and then went calmly on his way.

It was, therefore, quite in the order of things that Mr. Swinburne, being young and a poet, should be abused, and the critics set about it merrily, accusing him of indecency and immorality in his writings, and by means of garbled extracts torn from their context, and ingeniously misrepresented through the medium of their own prurient imaginations, raised a certain amount of prejudice against his works in the minds of those people who take their opinions at second-hand, and mistake cant and prudery for piety and purity.

It was in 1866, on the publication of his *Poems and Ballads*, that the attacks and misrepresentations reached their height, and Swinburne replied in a pamphlet, entitled *Notes on Poems and Reviews*, from which I take the following passages :-

"With regard to any opinion implied or expressed throughout my book, I desire that one thing should be remembered; the book is dramatic, many-faced, multifarious; and no utterance of enjoyment or despair, belief or unbelief, can properly be assumed as the assertion of its author's personal feeling or faith. Were each poem to be accepted as the deliberate outcome and result of the writer's conviction, not mine alone, but most other men's verses would leave nothing behind but a sense of cloudy chaos and suicidal contradiction.

"In one thing, indeed, it seems I have erred; I have forgotten to prefix to my work the timely warning of a great poet and humorist :-

" 'J'en préviens les mères des familles,

Ce que j'écris n'est pas pour les petites filles

Dont on coupe le pain en tartines; mes vers

Sont des vers de jeune homme."

"I have overlooked the evidence which every day makes clearer, that our time has room only for such as are content to write for children and girls. But this oversight is the sum of my offence.

"It would seem, indeed, as though to publish a book were equivalent to thrusting it with violence into the hands of every mother and nurse in the kingdom as fit and necessary food for female infancy. To all this, however, there is a grave side. The question at issue is wider than any between a single writer and his critics, or it might well be allowed to drop. It is this: whether or not the first and last requisite of art is to give no offence; whether or not all that cannot be lisped in the nursery is, therefore, to be cast out of the library; whether or not the domestic circle is to be for all men and writers the outer limit and extreme horizon of their world and work. For, to this we have come; and all students of art must face the matter as it stands. In no past century were artists ever bidden to work on these terms; nor are they now, except among us. With English versifiers now, the idyllic form is alone in fashion, the one great and prosperous poet of the time has given out the tune, and the hoarser choir takes it up.

"We have idylls good and bad, ugly and pretty; idylls of the farm and the mill; idylls of the dining-room and the deanery; idylls of the gutter and the gibbet.

"The idyllic form is best for domestic and pastoral poetry. It is naturally on a lower level than that of tragic or lyric verse. Its gentle and maidenly lips are somewhat narrow for the stream, and somewhat cold for the fire of song. *It is very fit for the sole diet of girls; not very fit for the sole sustenance of men.*"

The allusion in the above to the "idylls of the gutter and the gibbet" has been interpreted as applying to certain poems, *The Last of the Hangmen,* and *Nell,* written by Robert Buchanan, one of the most severe and unfair of Swinburne's critics, and when, shortly afterwards, the following verses appeared in the *Spectator,* they were generally ascribed to Buchanan.

"THE SESSION OF THE POETS.

"August, 1866.

"Di magni, salaputium disertum! - Cat. Lib. LIII.

I

"At the Session of Poets held lately in London,
　　The Bard of Freshwater was voted the chair:
With his tresses unbrush'd, and his shirt-collar undone,
　　He loll'd at his ease like a good-humour'd Bear;
'Come, boys!' he exclaimed, 'we'll be merry together!'
　　And lit up his pipe with a smile on his cheek;
While with eye like a skipper's cock'd up at the weather,
　　Sat the Vice-Chairman Browning, thinking in Greek.

II.

"The company gather'd embraced great and small bards,
　　Both strong bards and weak bards, funny and grave,
Fat bards and lean bards, little and tall bards,
　　Bards who wear whiskers, and others who shave.
Of books, men, and things, was the bards' conversation -
　　Some praised *Ecce Homo,* some deemed it so-so -
And then there was talk of the state of the nation,

95

And when the unwash'd would devour Mister Lowe.

III.

"Right stately sat Arnold, - his black gown adjusted
     Genteelly, his Rhine wine deliciously iced, -
With puddingish England serenely disgusted,
     And looking in vain (in the mirror) for 'Geist;'
He heark'd to the Chairman, with 'Surely!' and 'Really?'
     Aghast at both collar and cutty of clay, -
Then felt in his pocket, and breath'd again freely,
     On touching the leaves of his own classic play.

IV.

"Close at hand lingered Lytton, whose Icarus-winglets
     Had often betrayed him in regions of rhyme -
How glitter'd the eye underneath his gray ringlets,
     A hunger within it unlessened by time!
Remoter sat Bailey - satirical, surly -
     Who studied the language of Goethe too soon,
Who sang himself hoarse to the stars very early,
     And crack'd a weak voice with too lofty a tune.

V.

"How name all that wonderful company over? -
     Prim Patmore, mild Alford - and Kingsley also?
Among the small sparks who was realler than Lover?
     Among misses, who sweeter than Miss Ingelow?
There sat, looking mooney, conceited, and narrow,
     Buchanan, - who, finding when foolish and young,
Apollo asleep on a coster-girl's barrow,
     Straight dragged him away to see somebody hung.

VI.

"What was said? what was done? was there prosing or rhyming?
  Was nothing noteworthy in deed or in word?
Why, just as the hour for the supper was chiming,
  The only event of the evening occurred.
Up jumped, with his neck stretching out like a gander,
  Master Swinburne, and squeal'd, glaring out through his hair,
'All Virtue is bosh! Hallelujah for Landor!
  I disbelieve wholly in everything! - there!

VII.

"With language so awful he dared then to treat 'em, -
  Miss Ingelow fainted in Tennyson's arms,
Poor Arnold rush'd out, crying 'Soecl' inficetum!'
  And great bards and small bards were full of alarms;
Till Tennyson, flaming and red as a gipsy,
  Struck his fist on the table and uttered a shout:
'To the door with the boy! Call a cab! He is tipsy!'
  And they carried the naughty young gentleman out.

VIII.

"After that, all the pleasanter talking was done there-
  Whoever had known such an insult before?
The Chairman tried hard to re-kindle the fun there,
  But the Muses were shocked and the pleasure was o'er.
Then 'Ah!' cried the Chairman, 'this teaches me knowledge,
  The future shall find me more wise, by the powers!
This comes of assigning to yonkers from college
  Too early a place in such meetings as ours!"

                                          "Caliban.
"*The Spectator*, Sept. 15th, 1866."

97

Buchanan afterwards admitted that he had written these lines, and the circumstances leading up to that admission will be fully described in connection with his book on *The Fleshly School.*

To return, however, to Swinburne; his later poems differ from the earlier ones in having less of an amatory and more of a political cast, his ideas being of a strongly Republican order. His "Songs before Sunrise," were dedicated to Mazzini, the Italian patriot, who it was persuaded Swinburne not to plunge into the turbid stream of political life.

In his poems there is much that is obscure, almost unintelligible indeed; one critic epigrammatically remarked, "there is so much sound in Swinburne's songs, there is no room for sense, yet the sound alone is beautiful;" his verses are polished, and highly musical, either with a somewhat feverish *entrain*, or else deeply tinged with melancholy and despair.

ARTHUR W. E. O'SHAUGHNESSY

Was born in 1844, and at the age of twenty obtained (through the interest of Lord Lytton) a position in the Natural History Department of the British Museum. In 1873 he married Miss Eleanor Marston, who being the daughter and sister of poets, naturally had a bent in the direction of poetry, and assisted her husband in some of his early works, especially in a volume entitled "Toyland," which they published in 1875.

But Mrs. O'Shaughnessy and her two children all died in 1879, and the unfortunate young poet did not long survive them, he dying in London early in 1881.

His early books - "An Epic of Women" (1870); and "Lays of France" (1872) were successful, but "Music and Moonlight" (1874), was coldly received. After this he wrote a good many critical essays, and some translations from modern French poetry for the "Gentleman's Magazine." These were republished in a posthumous volume entitled "Songs of a Worker."

JONAS FISHER: A POEM IN BROWN & WHITE
AND
MR. ROBERT BUCHANAN

IN 1875, Messrs. Trübner published an anonymous work entitled "Jonas Fisher, a poem in Brown and White," which contained several passages strongly denouncing the so-called Fleshly School, and as Mr. Buchanan had already earned a notoriety for anonymously attacking rival poets; it seemed to some critics that this work might also be safely ascribed to his pen; the more especially as passages in it appeared to convey a meaning very similar to the sentiments already expressed by Buchanan in October, 1871, in the *Contemporary Review*, over the *nom de plume* of Thomas Maitland.

The following verses are part of a dialogue between the hero, Jonas Fisher, and Mr. Grace, in which the topics of Art and Poetry are discussed :-

> "It is not that our moderns lack
> All fiery essence in their mind;
> But what belongs to flesh and blood
> Appears to them so unrefined.

> "That to make simple manifold,
> And clear obscure, they take much pains -
> The grandsires wrote with all their hearts,
> The grandsons write with all their brains.

> " 'Well, Sir,' said I, 'I did not know
> That poets now took pains to be

So modest. Nay, I've heard them charged
     With very great indecency.'

" 'I did not speak so much of that,'
     Said he, 'the primness that I mean,
Is hating common manly force,
     Not hating things that are obscene.

" 'For (blameless held some noble names
     And placed on pinnacles above),
The moderns chiefly write with heart
     When writing about sensual love.'

" 'How pitiful, dear Sir,' said I,
     'The wanderings of the carnal man!
With such good subjects all around
     To pick and choose among, he can

" 'Debase himself to play with dirt!
     Now isn't it a *stupid* thing?'
Said he, 'I'm not so sure of that,
     The subject's always interesting.

" iI am not one of those who howl
     Whene'er the smallest word is said,
That might not fittingly appear
     In books to little children read.

" 'Nay, heart and soul, I do enjoy
     A good strong Rabelaisian shout
To crack my sides withal, the fun
     Rough rustics make o'er pipes and stout.

" 'A man's a man, not incense smoke
        To haunt a church and dread rude gales
And far too much for wholesome needs
        Mock modesty of speech prevails.

" 'Nor do I shudder over-much
        (However little I approve),
When men like Byron sing too free
        Of downright, honest, man-like love.

" 'But what my very soul abhors,
        What almost turns my blood to bile,
Is when some prurient paganist
        Stands up, and warbles with a smile

" 'A sick, putrescent, dulcet lay, -
        Like sugared sauce with meat too high, -
To hymn, or hint, the sensuous charms
        Of morbid immortality.

" 'Excuse me - do you think it right
        To read such poems, Mr. Grace?
Pray, did you ever meet with them
        In any reputable place?' "

The *Examiner* gave a criticism of this poem, in the course
of which it said -

"This anonymous poem is said to be the work of either
Mr. Robert Buchanan or the Devil; and delicate as man be the
question raised by this double-sided supposition, the weight of
probability inclines to the first of the alternatives. That the
author, whichever he is, is a Scotchman, may be inferred from

one or two incidental sneers at the characteristics of his countrymen. The worst things said about countries have been said by renegade natives. There are other and more specific circumstances which favour the report that Jonas Fisher is another of the aliases under which Mr. Buchanan is fond of challenging criticism, rather than one of the equally numerous disguises of the enemy.

"There is no reason why the Devil should go out of his way to abuse the 'Fleshly School.' Now the hero of this poem has views on some of the tendencies of modern poetry and art which coincide very closely with Mr. Buchanan's, exhibiting the same nicely-rounded and carefully-differentiated feelings of scorn for effeminate voluptuousness, and delight in that voluptuousness which is manly."

A few days after this somewhat ponderous criticism, there was a long letter in *The Examiner* entitled "The Devil's Due," this was signed "Thomas Maitland," the name over which, it will be remembered, Buchanan's attack on the Fleshly School in the *Contemporary Review* had originally appeared.

But this letter in *The Examiner* of December 11th, 1875, after ridiculing "Jonas Fisher," and comparing it to an inferior description of "Bab Ballads," proceeded to castigate Buchanan, whom it styled "multifaced idyllist of the gutter," (alluding to the number of the pseudonyms he had assumed, and to the low-life topics he had selected for his poems), on the assumption that he was its author, and to parody the letter he had written about his article in the *Contemporary*, in which he had stated that the *nom de plume* of Thomas Maitland was inserted by the publishers without his knowledge or consent, whilst he was away yachting in Scotland.

This is the satirical postscript affixed to the "Devil's Due" :-

"The writer being at present away from London on a cruise among the Philippine Islands in his steam yacht *The Skulk* (Captain Shuffleton, master), is, as can be proved on the oath or the solemn word of honour of the editor, publisher, and proprietor, responsible neither for an article which might with great foundation be attributed to Cardinal Manning or to Mr. Gladstone, or to any other writer in the *Contemporary Review* as its actual author; nor for the adoption of a signature under which his friends in general, acting not only without his knowledge, but against his expressed wishes on the subject, have thought it best and wisest to shelter his personal responsibility from any chance of attack. This frank, manly, and consistent explanation will, I cannot possibly doubt, make everything straight and safe on all hands."

Mr. Buchanan wrote a complain to *The Examiner* on the tone of this article, which it was afterwards admitted was written by Mr. Swinburne, who, it was said, was prepared to take the full responsibility. But Mr. Buchanan preferred to bring an action for libel against the proprietor of *The Examiner*, Mr. P. A. Taylor, M. P. for Leicester, who pleaded not guilty, and also set up the defence that the alleged libels were only fair criticisms upon the defendant's works.

The case was tried before Mr. Justice Archibald and a special jury in June, 1876, and resulted in a verdict for the plaintiff with £150 damages. Much amusement was caused during the trial by the cross-examination of the plaintiff and his witnesses, the first of whom was Lord Southesk, who appeared to claim "Jonas Fisher" as his work, in which he admitted that he had expressed his views against the "Fleshly School," consisting principally of the works of Mr. Swinburne, Mr. D. G. Rossetti,

Mr. Morris and Mr. Arthur O'Shaughnessy.

The Earl of Southesk was called, and stated - "I am the author of the work called 'Jonas Fisher.' My work contains nothing whatever against the characteristic virtues of the Scottish people. In the poem I express my honest views of the writings of the Fleshly School. I have only had Mr. Buchanan's acquaintance since the beginning of the present year."

"Jonas Fisher is supposed to be a City missionary in Edinburgh, writing on the Scotch people, and visiting amongst the poorer classes. There is nothing which offends decency in my work, but it is not a *poem* written for boys and girls, because I speak plainly of things, but there is no immorality in it."[6]

---

[6] I have recently been favoured with the following communication from the Earl of Southesk, explaining his position with regard to the trial arising from the criticisms on "Jonas Fisher" :-

"I am obliged by your letter; probably, should we ever meet, you would find that your own ideas and mine are not very different. Through accidental circumstances my name was prominently connected with that of Mr. Buchanan - a gentleman with whom I am but slightly acquainted - and (to my knowledge) I am supposed to be an adherent of any set or party to which he may belong, at all events to be an opponent of the Art Movement.

"My life-long intimacy with the founder of the Grosvenor Gallery has not prevented this misconception.

"Yet if you would once again refer to 'Jonas Fisher,' Part III., verses 188-225, you would see my views plainly set down, and surely without a touch of approval of anything approaching to prudery or puritanism.

"The whole book is meant as a protest against narrowness of view.

"It never was my intention to assail any individual or any party except on the grounds of some special offence against what seems to me good art as well as good morals - in the wide, not the puritanical, sense.

"I do not retract one word in 'Jonas Fisher' - my object is to remove misconception of my aims and motives.'

Then came the plaintiff, Mr. Robert Buchanan, who stated that he had been a literary man for 15 years, that he had written the article entitled "The Fleshly School," having given instructions that it should be published anonymously, to which Messrs. Strahan objected, and affixed the name "Thomas Maitland" to it, without his knowledge. When "Jonas Fisher" was afterwards ascribed to him, he had written to repudiate its authorship, although he admitted he had written other anonymous poems severely attacking Mr. Swinburne and others, as, for instance, in the "Session of Poets," published in 1866. At that time he had never seen Mr. Swinburne, although in the poem he ridiculed his personal appearance and manner; and he stated generally that he lavished about as much abuse on Mr. Swinburne, Mr. Rossetti, and others of the "Fleshly School," as he could put his pen to.

In the defence objection was taken to Mr. Buchanan asserting himself as an authority, and constituting himself the censor of the morals of England, and on the ground that he, too, had written works of questionable decency and of doubtful morality, such as "Liz," "The Little Milliner," "The Last of the Hangmen," and "Nell" - from which various extracts were read out in court, as also the following passage from "The White Rose and Red" :-

> "Till with passionate sensation,
> Body and brain began to burn,
> And he yielded to the bursting,
> Burning, blinding, hungering, thirsting
> Passion felt by breasts and men!
> And his eyes caught love and rapture,
> And he held her close in capture,
> Kissing lips that kiss'd again."

And another of a still more questionable kind from a poem entitled "The Nuptial Song," which closes thus :-

> "As freely as maids give a lock away,
> She gave herself unto him;
> What was the bridegroom? Clay, common clay,
> Yet the wild joy slipt through him.
> He kissed her lips, he drank her breath in bliss,
> He drew her to his bosom -
> As a clod kindles at the Spring's first kiss,
> His being burst to blossom."

Mr. Hawkins, Q. C., who appeared for the defence, said to the jury :-

"I shall ask you to consider whether the works of Mr. Buchanan have made for him that mark in the literature of his country as to entitle him to make the attacks he has made upon Rossetti and Swinburne. How does he begin? He produces the 'Session of Poets,' and introduces Mr. Swinburne. Here is a poem written in 1866, in which Mr. Robert Buchanan professes to bring together the leading British poets. There are a good many of them, but if you take in the first rank a round dozen it is saying a good deal, and Mr. Robert Buchanan immediately dots himself down in the first rank of the dozen, and no doubt in the 'Session of Poets' he could with much greater brilliancy have taken the chair at that literary assembly than Alfred Tennyson himself.

"This, gentlemen, is the poet who has made his mark in the literature of his country! Mr. Gladstone must have thought highly of him when he granted him a pension, but I do not know whether Mr. Gladstone had previously read the classic effusion I have quoted, or his "Liz," or his "Little Milliner," or even "The Last of the Hangmen." Well, if you do not call this the 'idyllist of the gutter,' I don't know where you will find one.

"Thus, in one poem, I find a coster girl, who lived in the neighbourhood of St. Giles's, and fell into a difficulty with a gentleman, who himself pursued a course of life which ultimately brought him to the gallows. Another poem is entitled 'Liz.' Here is the life of a wretchedly poor girl, who has been seduced by one of the low persons who inhabit the same classical locality I have already mentioned, and who has got an illegitimate child. These are the stories in which Mr. Robert Buchanan delights. He has used hard words of other people, and, considering the things that he had written himself, he could hardly complain if some people thought fit also to pull them to pieces."

It was also contended that Mr. Buchanan had gravely transgressed the bounds of decorum in his personal attacks upon Mr. Swinburne, notably in the lines :-

"Up jumped, with his neck stretching out like a gander,
　　Master Swinburne, and squeal'd glaring out thro' his hair,
All virtue is bosh! Hallelujah for Landor!
　　I disbelieve wholly in everything! - there!"

and further on, where he accuses him of being carries out of the meeting in a tipsy condition. Then, as the judge pointed out, Mr. Buchanan's mode of criticising the poets of the "Fleshly School" was calculated to do more harm than good, he having availed himself of the opportunity to quote much that was lewd and reprehensible in the poems, and in fact, he added, he thought it a great pity the case had ever come into court, as it was not credible to either party.

So far as Mr. Buchanan is concerned there is little more to note. He has written some poems and novels, and is the author of two pieces, "The Shadow of the Sword," and "Lucy Brandon," (founded on the late Lord Lytton's "Paul Clifford,") both of which were withdrawn from the boards after very brief careers.

The critics condemned "The Shadow of the Sword" as a tedious bombastic production, unworthy of serious consideration. Mr. Buchanan naturally resented these unfavourable remarks, and accused Mr. John Coleman (who produced the piece at the Olympic Theatre), of having grievously mutilated the drama, stating also that he had been personally befooled and impoverished.

Mr. John Coleman replied that the alterations made had received Mr. Buchanan's full assent, and that he had paid Mr. Buchanan every shilling of the purchase money agreed upon prior to the production of the play.

Two things only are certain - that the play was a failure, and that Mr. Buchanan was very angry with the London dramatic critics, who are incapable, as he asserts, of either civility or fair play.

As to "Lucy Brandon," which was brought out at the Imperial and suddenly withdrawn, the author wrote that its withdrawal "was entirely unconnected with its dramatic success or failure," but a successful piece generally has a run of more than a few days.

To a sensitive nature possessing highly-strung nerves, the discordant vibrations of adverse criticism are, no doubt, distressing; Mr. Buchanan appears to possess unusually susceptible feelings, and what is still more unfortunate for him, to be incapable of concealing or suppressing them.

Hence no sooner does an uncomplimentary notice appear of one of his productions than he writes to prove that the critic is in the wrong, and knows nothing of the subject in hand.

Critics usually *are* in the wrong, and, being mere mortals, cannot know, even a little, about everything.

But the public perfectly understand all this, and make allowances accordingly, whilst every publisher knows that in so far as influencing the sale of a novel or a poem the value of a criticism is often enhanced by its being of an unfavourable description, particularly if it asserts that the work contains a dash of impropriety. An historical or scientific book may be damned by one strong and ably-written condemnatory review, but not a poem, a novel, or a play, else few, even of the best would have survived, as Mr. Buchanan ought to know, for he himself has written some of the most unsparing criticisms of exactly those works which are now most popular. In his last novel, "The Martyrdom of Madeline," he has bitterly satirised the editors of two society journals under the thinly-veiled names of *Lagardère* and *Edgar Yahoo*, the latter being described as the "social *chiffonier* of his age" raking for garbage in the filth of the street and in the sewers; whilst Lagardère is painted as a profligate, boastful, ignorant, lying, cowardly monster, often whipped and universally despised. Yet when this same novel was noticed in *The Academy* and the reviewer, in a mild manner, expostulated with the author on the tone of his book as belying the promises of purity contained in its preface, and for attacking other men of genius under transparent transliterated names, Mr. Buchanan was not content to accept the criticism which allowed him to be a man of genius and reputation, and strongly excited curiosity as to the contents of his novel, but wrote to the editor complaining that he had long been subjected to literary persecution, adding "Though rudely assailed, I have at least published a description of my persecutors."

He compares himself to Don Quixote attacking the windmills, but the simile is unfortunate, for we nowhere read that the chivalrous knight complained afterwards of the windmills' treatment of him. So long as Mr. Buchanan continues to tilt at the windmills of the press, so long must he expect hard blows and heavy falls, and it would be wiser and more dignified not to complain of the wounds obtained in the fray. What, however, chiefly concerns us in this matter is the somewhat remarkable statements contained in this letter, concerning the poets of the Aesthetic School, and in justice to Mr. Buchanan I will insert those paragraphs in full, premising that the reviewer had accused him of satirising D. G. Rossetti, under the pseudonym "Blanco Serena," and or renewing his attacks on his old enemies, the fleshly poets. On these points Mr. Buchanan's language is clear and distinct, and is highly credible, as a handsome acknowledgement of the merits of some with whom he was supposed to be at enmity.

"Your reviewer may distrust my motives, he should at least be accurate in his description of my performances. He accuses me, in the first place, of attacking my 'old friends the fleshly poets.' Who are the fleshly poets, so-called? If your reviewer refers to Mr. Swinburne, to Mr. Morris, to Mr. Rossetti, and to those whom I once classed as their disciples, I beg leave to re-assert (in addition to the disclaimer in my Preface) that my satire concerns not *them*, though it may, I suppose, have a certain retrospective application to writings which wee merely a phase of their genius. Mr. Swinburne has long left the pastoral region shepherded by the impeccable Gautier; he has risen to heights of clear and beautiful purpose, where I gladly do homage to him. Mr. Morris may be passed by without a word; he needs no apology of mine. Mr. Rossetti, I freely admit now, never was a fleshly poet at all; never, at any rate, fed upon the poisonous honey of French art. Who, then, remains to complain of misinterpretation? If your reviewer had said that I satirized Gautier and his school of pseudo-aesthetics, and their possible pupils in his country, he would have been within his right.

"One word more. Your reviewer insinuates (there is no mistaking his innuendo) that a certain character in my story is a shadow-picture of the late Mr. Dante Rossetti. To show the injustice of this supposition, I will simply ask your readers to compare the lineaments of my Blanco Serena, a society-hunting, worldly-minded, insincere, but good-humoured, *fashionable painter*, with the literary image of Mr. Rossetti, a solitude-loving, unworldly, thoroughly sincere and earnest, if sometimes saturnine, man of genius, *in revolt against society*. I wish to have no mistake on this, to me, very solemn matter. What I wrote of Mr. Rossetti, ten years ago, stands. What I wrote of Mr. Rossetti in the inscription of *God and the Man* also stands. Time brings about its revenges, Can the least acute observer of literature have failed to notice that the so-called fleshly school, in proportion as it has grown saner, purer, and more truly impassioned in the cause of humanity, has lost its hold upon the so-called fleshly public - even on the dapper master-millers and miller's men of the journals of nepotism and malignity? Certain of our critics said to certain of our poets - 'Go that way; there lies the short cut to immortality. But the poets, after going a few paces, paused, recognising, as only true poets can recognise, the easy descent to Acheron."

This letter appeared in *The Academy*, July 1st, 1882.

As closing this unpleasant controversy, Mr. T. Hall Caine, in his "Recollections of Rossetti," gives the following communication he had recently received from Mr. R. Buchanan :-

"In perfect frankness, let me say a few words concerning our old quarrel. While admitting that my article in the *Contemporary Review* was unjust to Rossetti's claims as a poet, I have ever held, and still hold, that it contained nothing to warrant the manner in which it was received by the poet and his circle.

"At the time it was written the newspapers were full of panegyric; mine was a mere drop of gall in an ocean of *eau sucrée*.

"That it could have had on any man the effect you describe, I can scarcely believe; indeed, I think that no living man had so little to complain of as Rossetti, on the score of criticism. Well, my protest was received in a way which turned irritation into wrath, wrath into violence; and then ensued the paper war which lasted for years. If you compare what I have written of Rossetti with what his admirers have written of myself, I think you will admit that there has been some cause for *me* to complain, to shun society, to feel bitter against the world; but happily, I have a thick epidermis, and the courage of an approving conscience. I was unjust, as I have said; most unjust when I impugned the purity and misconceived the passion of writings too hurriedly read and reviewed *currente calamo*: but I was at least honest and fearless, and wrote with no personal malignity. Save for the action of the literary defence, if I may so term it, my article would have been as ephemeral as the mood which induced its composition. I make full admission of Rossetti's claims to the purest kind of literary renown, and if I were to criticise his poems *now*, I should write very differently. But nothing will shake *my* conviction that the cruelty, the unfairness, the pusillanimity, has been on the other side, not on mine. The *amenae* of my Dedication in *God and the Man* was a sacred thing; between *his* spirit and mine: not between my character and the cowards who have attacked it. I thought he would understand - which would have been, and indeed is, sufficient. I cried, and cry, no truce with the horde of slanderers who hid themselves within his shadow. That is all. But when all is said, there still remains the pity that our quarrel should ever have been. Our little lives are too short for such animosities. Your friend is at peace with God - that God who will justify and cherish him, who has dried his tears, and who will turn the shadow of his sad life-dream into full sunshine. My only regret is that we did not meet - that I did not take him by the hand; but I am old-fashioned enough to believe that this world is only a prelude, and that our meeting may take place yet."

Just a short time before his death Rossetti had heard of Buchanan's retraction of he charges involved in the article on the "Fleshly School," and was strangely touched by the pathetic dedication to him of Buchanan's romance, *God and the Man* :-

TO AN OLD ENEMY.

I would have snatch's a bay leaf from thy brow,
Wronging the chaplet on an honoured head;
In peace and charity I bring thee now
A lily flower instead.

Pure as thy purpose, blameless as thy song,
Sweet as thy spirit, may this offering be;
Forget the bitter blame that did thee wrong,
And take the gift from me!

In a later edition (after the death of Rossetti), the following verses were added to the dedication :-

To Dante Gabriel Rossetti
Calmly, thy royal robe of death around thee,
Thou sleepest, and weeping brethren round thee stand,
Gently they placed, ere yet God's angel crowned thee,
My lily in thy hand!

I never knew thee living, O my brother!
But on thy breast my lily of love now lies;
And by that token, we shall know each other,
When God's voice saith, "Arise!"

That Mr. Buchanan means well there can be no doubt; he, at least, is on the side of the angels; if he will be a little more tolerant of others, and learn to chafe less under the lash of the critics, he will win public opinion over to his side, and then he may defy the reviewers to do their worst. But of all things the British public most dislike a man with a grievance.

PUNCH'S ATTACKS ON THE AESTHETES

THE trial of Buchanan v. Taylor being over, the "Jonas Fisher" controversy was soon forgotten, and for several years the Aesthetic School enjoyed a tolerable immunity from similar attacks. In a quiet, unostentatious, but most effective manner, it was gaining converts; its canons of criticism, and its dictates in matters of taste were being largely adopted by the cultivated of both sexes, and its influence on art, poetry, dress, and furniture, was visible in every direction.

Then it was that Mr. Du Maurier took the subject up in the pages of *Punch*, and commenced a series of caricatures which one would imagine to be grossly exaggerated but that, as all the world knows, the talented artist is so great a favourite with the aristocracy that his representations of the dukes and duchesses, lords and ladies, constantly appearing in *Punch*, must needs to be truthful and correct, as he spends the greater part of his life in the study of such exalted personages in their own elegant saloons and boudoirs. It is to be a little regretted that it is so, for to the general run of Englishmen, who have not the *entrée* to such select society, it savours somewhat of toadyism, this constant reference to titled persons and exclusive society; besides, the subject becomes somewhat monotonous, especially as all the ladies are so very much alike, and the fun, what of it there is, is of such an extremely refined drawing-room description.

By way of an introduction into what our French friends call *Le High Life*, I quote one of Mr. Du Maurier's latest sketches, and leave the intelligent reader to form his own opinion as to the possibility of such a dialogue (*probability* being entirely out of the question).

"Mrs Ponsonby de Tomkyn's Loses her Temper. - Mrs. P. de T.'s Last New Duchess (graciously unbending): "When I came here before, Madame Gaminot was here; but she wouldn't sing - she 'took her hook,' as Cadbury called it - went away, you know!" Mrs. P. de T.: "Yes; and so did your Grace and Lord Cadbury, in consequence." Her Grace: "A - just so. Who's that very funny person talking to Mr. Whatshisname - Thingummy you know - your clever *writing* friend, from America? Is *she* a comic singer, and will she sing?" Mrs. P. de T.: "No, I don't think she'll *sing*. That very funny person is my friend, Lady Midas." Her Grace (who always speaks her mind) "What! And pray, Mrs. Tompkyns, are there no *ladies* left in England, that *I* should be asked here to dine with the wife of a successful *sausage maker?*" Mrs. P. de T.: "You were asked here to dine with Mr. Whatshisname, duchess - (Thingummy, you know)! You yourself asked me to ask you to meet him; and I am only too glad to have such an opportunity of showing my clever writing friend from America that there *are* some ladies still left in England, and very *great* ladies too" - (Her Grace bows stiffly) - "who can't even behave as decently as a *sausage-maker's* wife! But perhaps your Grave would prefer to - a - take your Grave's hook? Shall I ring and order your carriage?" [Her Grace reflects that her carriage is gone - loses her head - stammers - dines - apologises, and is quite civil to Lady Midas after dinner.]

Punch makes one sigh at times for the manly style and fresh breezy humour of John Leech, bold, vigorous, and thoroughly English, whose girls were real, merry, healthy, laughing, jolly girls, not the sickly, namby-pamby, over-dressed, all-alike-at-the-price, young ladies of Mr. Du Maurier, whose ideal of female beauty

117

consists of one stereotyped face at the top of an abnormally tall and slender figure. It is no exaggeration to say that in proportion to the accessories in his pictures, the ladies must frequently stand over six feet in height, and that the rules of perspective are entirely ignored.

The latter failing is so constant that it probably arises from a defect of vision. A few weeks since there was a full page drawing in *Punch* with the title: "Not fond of steering! - Just ain't we, though!" The epigraph was a trifle slangy; yet the picture was full of animation, but how about perspective? Some one writing to *The Illustrated London News* thus worked it out :-

"Taking the height of the lady pulling 'stroke' in her slightly bent attitude as only five feet, ad fixing the gentleman in the stern (whose knees, only, appear) as the spectator, I work on the represented size of the lady in the bows, and make the distance between the stroke and bows to be twenty-seven and a half feet. Allowing for the distance from the prow and stern to the two rowers mentioned, the craft cannot measure less than from fifty to fifty-four feet from stern to stern; while the width of beam is about five feet."

We must, however, for the want of a better, accept Du Maurier as the leading Society artist on *Punch*.

John Tenniel confines himself to the cartoons which, though they are frequently highly finished, have not the same vigour they had some years since, and for political ideas simply embody the ever-changing moods expressed in the leaders of the *Times* newspaper.

Linley Sambourne's style is peculiar, and only fitted to delineate the odd fancies of his own brain; clever, quaint, and original they are, but they are not *Society* pictures.

Charles Keene does well, and would do better in this branch of art, if his execution only equalled his conception. His ideas are frequently humorous and funny, but his drawing is hopelessly scratchy and muddled, many of his faces being destitute of any human expression whatever, whilst occasionally the features are missing altogether, nothing but the outlines being visible.

So, for the Society sketches, Du Maurier takes the lead, and it cannot be denied that some of his drawings are highly finished representations of those refined and cultivated, but somewhat foolish members of Society, who imagine that the world was created for their especial benefit, and that nothing is worthy of one moment's consideration that is outside the narrow range of the Peerage, and that *no one* can be *any one* whose name is not included in that magic list of the Upper Ten Thousand. His scope is limited, his subjects monotonous, and his humour, what little there is of it, is of a mildly conventional and eminently respectable type.

It is quite in accordance with the traditions of *Punch* to attack the Aesthetic movement: from the first it has been a combative journal; at one time, through ridiculing the Roman Catholic religion (a topic which *gentlemen* do not usually jest about), it lost one of its best contributors, namely Richard Doyle. Then in 1847 it savagely satirized Alfred Bunn, or "Poet Bunn," as he was styled (the author of "I dreamt that I dwelt in marble halls," "When other lips and other hearts," &c.) but Bunn was not easily frightened; he issued a paper entitled "A Word with *Punch*," in which he dealt such hard and telling blows that henceforth *Mr. Punch* finding discretion better than valour, ceased his attacks on the "Hot cross Bunn."

A Word with Punch, by Alfred Bunn, dated November, 1847, consisted of 12 pages the same size as *Punch*, and with a frontispiece which singularly resembled that of the *Punch* of that time, but on closer examination it is seen that Mr. Punch is in the pillory, surrounded by the celebrities of the day.

The articles it contains are especially severe upon Douglas Jerrold, Gilbert à Beckett and Mark Lemon (then the principal contributors to *Punch*), who are respectively styled, Wronghead, Sleekhead, and Thickhead.

The draughtsman employed by Mr. Bunn to illustrate the paper was no mean caricaturist, Mark Lemon is shown as a pot boy (it is said he once kept a small public house).

The savagely sarcastic Douglas Jerrold appears as a serpent; a man he was, as Bunn says, of undoubted genius, but sarcastic, spiteful and vindictive.

Gilbert à Beckett is attired in a lawyer's gown and wig, with a demon's tail and hoofs. Mr. Bunn enumerates the number of small rubbishing papers G. à B. had edited, described his unsuccessful lesseeship of the Fitzroy Theatre, Fitzroy Street, Tottenham Court Road, and cites the petition to the Insolvent Debtors Court, in which G. à B. described himself as *formerly* a gentleman, afterwards an editor, as if the two were incompatible.

Mr. Bunn asserts that the circulation of *Punch* had once reached 70,000, but that it was then only 30,000, and he concludes his paper thus :- "Your puppets, who have assailed, ridiculed, and caricatured me for years, *without* any reason whatever, will not in common consistency, abandon this branch of their trade now I have given them reason; and without thinking what cause they have given *me*, will go again at their dirty work.

"In that case, I am prepared to pay back any compliment I receive with the highest rate of interest allowed by law, and shall let you, and perhaps them, into a secret or two worth knowing."

On the back are burlesque advertisements of the period, and at the foot a pill and draught with the label :-

"This dose to be repeated should the patients require it.

Wronghead,

Sleekhead,

Thickhead."

Prefixed to the copy in the British Museum is the following note signed by the Antiquary, *F. W. Fairholt.*

"This severe piece of personality was deservedly called forth by the unjustifiable attacks made by the *Punch* writers on Bunn. He appears only to have been guilty of not flattering their vanity sufficiently, or employing them as authors; daring also to write librettos for Balfe's operas (Bunn being connected with Covent Garden and Drury Lane). Unfortunately for them he knew too much of their antecedents; and after much provocation, produced this pamphlet. It was a conclusive blow, and they never afterwards attacked him. It was too true to be pleasant, and has been industriously bought up and destroyed, so that it is now very scarce."

The next individual chosen as the butt for its pitiless scorn was Prince Albert, whose appearance, public actions, and broken English came in for many personal attacks, which were no doubt prompted by good taste against a well-meaning foreigner, whose high position prevented him from retaliating, and whose cultivated tastes and efforts towards the improvement of the people, and the dress of the soldiers, offered splendid targets for satire, and careful, consistent, and long-continued misrepresentation.

Lord Beaconsfield's Jewish birth, his somewhat singular personal appearance, and his little harmless fopperies, also lent themselves admirably to caricature; and so, throughout the chapter, the shafts of ridicule have been levelled first at one and then at another of the leading men of the time, including Lord Brougham, for his ugliness, and the late Harrison Ainsworth and Lord Lytton (then Sir Edward Bulwer-Lytton) for their good looks.

Once, when *Punch* had grossly insulted the late Lord Mayo, the *Globe* struck a heavy blow at his folly and indecency, concluding the article by asking :-

"Why should *Punch* pretend to be a comic publication? The answers will no doubt be various. Some will say because it *once had* a Jerrold and a Thackeray on its staff. But and alas! Punch's own pages prove that Jerrold and Thackeray are dead. Shall *Punch* be famous as a wit because Burnand can be boisterous, because Brooks are Shallow, or because it takes nine Tailors to make a man? We, too, give it up. Only we would say, that we regret the years which bring us our friend *Punch* in a form which compels us to say, he has only such politics as consistent in the vulgarization of *The Times*, and that he is, *when not feebly spiteful, simply inane.*"

However much these, and other spiteful and personal attacks, may have helped the circulation of *Punch* (for the vulgar herd like to see their betters turned to scorn), they cannot be said to have increased its reputation, and when brave old George Cruikshank was asked, not once, but several times, to contribute to its pages, he replied, "No; I never had had, and never will have anything to do with it," and he never did, for no single line from the pencil of the greatest humorist of the century ever appeared in *Punch*.

Our American Cousins, with their keen sense of humour,

and intense, but quiet appreciation for the truly *witty*, are constantly remarking upon the dearth of really comic writing in our periodicals. The *New York Tribune* observed some time since :-

"Upon examining a number of the professionally comic newspapers which are printed in London, we have been surprised to observe how little wit or humour appears to satisfy the English public. We found in *Punch*, in *Judy*, and in *Fun*, hardly anything except puns. A fatal objection to this species of drollery is, that it speedily becomes intolerably tiresome, not less in print than in conversation, and thus defeats in the most dismal way its own facetious purpose. A pun, which is no more than a pun, and which does not include that suggestion of likeness in incongruity which is the essence of wit, is really worthless, and quite within the capacity of the dullest of mortals. This is irritating enough in colloquial intercourse; but there are some half-a-dozen weekly journals in London which make it their whole business to furnish puns to the British public, and do that business with a reckless and truly astonishing disregard of sense and literary decency."

Surely Macaulay must have been fresh from reading a number of *Punch*, when he wrote -

"A wise man *might* talk like this by his own fireside; but that any human being, after having made such jokes, should write them down, copy them out, and transmit them to the printer, correct the proof-sheets, and send them forth into the world, is enough to make us ashamed of our species."

But humorists and satirists, taken as a whole, are a miserably weekly set now-a-days. Caricature, which was once a deadly weapon, is not but another means of advertising, and so far from being withered by the pictures (and they are at times pretty pictures) published about them, Aesthetes have only flourished the more, and they now openly avow and practise that Aestheticism which previously they felt almost bound to restrain within their own immediate circle of acquaintances.

The Aesthetic business having drawn so well in the pages of a comic paper, it was not surprising that two theatres should proceed to ridicule Aestheticism. There is one curious incident in this connection which should not be passed over. This is, that the authors who supplied these two theatres were at mortal enmity because one forestalled the other with regard to what both of them believed to be a great original notion, the notion of making fun out of the Aesthetic Movement. Perhaps it was original, as originality goes in these times. If so, originality may well walk hand in hand with comicality - I mean the comicality of the comic papers.

> "Then stood a senile God upon the floor,
> Who used to keep Hoeprintus in a roar,
> But who, grown old and feeble, could not last,
> Save for his reputation in the past.
> Gone are his Wits, his Leech that once we saw
> (And what a splendid Leech he was to draw),
> His Jerrold, Thackeray, his Mayhew, Hood,
> His Lemon, too, and it is understood
> That without Lemon, Punch cannot be good;
> But still the God, for humour once renowned,
> Essayed to speak. His voice in groans was drowned;
> Loud shout the Gods, his prosiness to baulk,
> 'We'll see your pictures, but you must not talk.'
> So, sat the aged and effete Buffoon,
> Content to circulate his last cartoon."

But since the above lines were written, some years ago, even *Punch's* cartoons have lost their power to interest or amuse, whilst they are occasionally in execrable taste, as for instance was that published the week following the assassination of Lord Frederick Cavendish, when Tenniel could find no topic more appropriate than a silly sneer at Mr. Forster, who was represented as frightened away from Ireland by assassins. Not only was the portrait of Mr. Forster miserably drawn, but to represent him as leaving his perilous duties in Ireland, through fear of his enemies, was a gross libel on the former Chief Secretary, who had boldly visited the most disturbed districts of Ireland, and had exposed himself fearlessly in the midst of yelling crowds and hostile natives.

If these things were witty, one might pardon their spite, but as Disraeli wrote some years since, "Cannot you keep your friend *Punch* in order? He gets malevolent without being playful." This is the explanation of his waning influence, and if I have been somewhat severe in my comments upon *Punch*, I have but to draw attention to his persistent attacks upon everything connected with the Aesthetic Movement to prove justification. Admitted that some *foolish* people affect the style and the dress, and exaggerate the tone, it cannot be denied that true Aestheticism has worked a vast amount of good, and to continue to sneer at those who originated the movement, does not prove them to be in the wrong, but goes to show that he who sneers is a somewhat prejudiced, ignorant, and foolish individual.

When one thinks of the great work that was done by caricaturists and comic writers in the days that are gone, it is difficult to help blushing for the stuff that is now regarded as caricature and comic writing. Hogarth and Gillray, Rowlandson, Cruikshank, and "H. B.," Rabelais, Swift and Sterne, Smollett and Defoe, are in these days voted coarse and common, also; but the work they did was of vast benefit to the community. Without its coarseness and its commonness, so also was the work done a generation ago by John Leech and Douglas Jerrold, by Albert Smith, Richard Doyle and William Makepeace Thackeray. If anyone turns to the earliest and best days of *Punch*, he will find it devoted to the consideration of subjects which would not for a moment be tolerated in its present superfine pages. The *Punch* which paved the way for its effeminate namesake of to-day would be voted vulgar, personal, and scurrilous now, and unfit for the perusal of the very genteel classes. Still, it served its purpose, and made the paper so powerful that its bygone reputation can now be safely traded upon by a staff of twaddlers, and plagiarists, artistic and literary.

Punch is now but a poor feeble old man, who makes a great parade of his highly-refined feelings, his polished manners, and his classical education, never losing an opportunity to introduce a Greek or Latin quotation, whilst always sneering at any luckless author who should happen to do the same. Indeed, if there is one thing more than another that the Punch contributors pride themselves on, it is their knowledge of foreign languages, a knowledge which is useful, so far as it goes, as it enables them occasionally to *borrow* a little joke from the French or German comic papers; and having exhausted every witticism that the poor weak English language is capable of, they fall back (like Spanish cows) upon French, and this is their idea of

LIGHT REFRESHMENT.

(For the Devotees of Sweetness and Light)

An Aesthetic Menu

Lis en branches au naturel.

Fleurs de tournesol à l'oriflamme.

Poissons louches à la dado.

Cuisse de cicogne tour au long.

Tête d'épouvantail à la Botticelli.

Compote de fruit défendu à la Baudelaire fortement sucrée.

After Mr. Du Maurier had pretty well used up the subject of the Aesthetic School in a somewhat impersonal and not unkindly manner, the editor took up the topic, and having a French play (Le Mari à la Campagne) to work on as a foundation, he borrowed some good situations from an old play entitled "The Serious Family," and by making "The Colonel" an American, with a Yankee twang (a character which entirely depends for its success upon the actor who represents it), with the witty remark, "Why, cert'nly," to be repeated *ad libitum* and *ad nauseaum*, he manufactures a play, which (after some difficulty with the incredulous managers) was produced, and owing to the popular interest in Aestheticism, obtained a success its own intrinsic merits would never have obtained for it.

The history of *The Colonel* is peculiar. On Monday, the third of June, 1844, a new comedy in three acts was produced at the Théatre Francais, Paris, entitled *Le Mari à la Campagne*.

This amusing piece (written by Messrs. Bayard and J. De Wailly) proved a success, and naturally it attracted the attention of English managers. It was admirably translated by Mr. Morris Barnett, and under the title of *The Serious Family*, was produced at the Haymarket Theatre in 1849, when the late J. B. Buckstone performed the part of the canting hypocrite *Aminadab Sleek*, upon which character Mr. Burnand modelled his *Lambert Streyke*. In fact, in reading *The Serious Family* one cannot but be struck with the audacity of the production of *The Colonel* as an original piece; scene for scene, in some instances word for word, does

Mr. Burnand follow Mr. Barnett. The leading motive only is altered; in the original the hero is driven from home by the melancholy puritanical nature of his surroundings, a very probable assumption, whereas in *The Colonel* the same result is brought about by the Aesthetic mania of the hero's wife and mother-in-law, which is an absurdity, for Aestheticism cannot but lend to beautify a home and render it more attractive to its occupants. Here is a comparison of the casts of the two plays :-

The characters in Mr. Morris Barnett's, The Serious Family, 1849.	Their counterparts in Mr. Barnand's *original* comedy, *The Colonel*, 1881.
Charles Torrens.	Richard Forrester.
Captain Murphy Maguire (an Irishman).	Colonel W. W. Woodd (a Yankee).
Frank Vincent.	Edward Langton.
Aminadab Sleek.	Lambert Streyke.
Danvers.	Mullins.
Lady Creamly.	Lady Tompkins.
Mrs. C. Torrens.	Mrs. Forrester.
Emma Torrens.	Nellie Forrester.
Mrs. Delmaine.	Mrs. Blyth.
Graham (her maid).	Goodall (her maid).
	Basil Giorgione (Streyke's nephew).[7]

Here is an American notice of it taken from Puck of last January :-

" 'The Colonel,' at Abbey's Park Theatre, was a great disappointment to everybody. Not that Mr. Wallack is to blame,

---

[7] A small part created by Mr. Barnand. The other characters are simply re-named, the amusing Irish Captain of the original being transformed into the Yankee Colonel.

for he does what is expected of him; but the play is nothing more than an unblushing appropriation of another man's work. The French original, 'Le Mari a la Campagne,' is, of course, at everybody's service, but the author of 'The Serious Family' exhausted its possibilities for the English-speaking stage in the best manner. It is, then, rather cool, to say the least of it, for Mr. F. C. Burnand, the editor of our venerable and funereal contemporary, *Punch*, to call 'The Colonel' *his* play, when he has simply altered the dialogue, here and there, of another play, and made impossible aesthetes of what, in the original, were possible religious enthusiasts. Mr. Burnand, in spite of his reputation, by this work can certainly lay no claim to be considered either a wit or a playwright, and his ideas of dramatic construction are evidently of the crudest and most controversial character. 'Why, certn'ly,' repeated at intervals, is not sufficient to make an original play, although Mr. Burnand thinks that it is. The scenery was good, and the acting, as a whole indifferent, although Miss Rachel Sanger played her part in an attractive manner. The British importations who took the other characters did not impress us by their finish or excellence."

But how plainly do these American writers show their small knowledge of English character in writing thus.

What *does* the British public *care* for the intrinsic merit of a poem, a picture or a play - if Royalty does but single it out for a passing word of recognition, its name is made, and the poet, artist, actress, playwright, or music-hall singer, at once becomes famous. So with *The Colonel*, what was most vaunted in its enormous and ubiquitous advertisements? Its originality - No! Its comicality - No! Its truth to nature - No! - Mr. Burnand and Mr. Edgar Bruce knew which was their trump card, and they played it, thus :-

"THE COLONEL."
By F. C. Burnand.

Mr. Edgar Bruce, at the invitation of their Royal Highnesses the Prince and Princess of Wales, gave a Special Representation of "The Colonel," with his Company, at Abergeldie Castle, on Tuesday, October 4th, 1881. The Performance was honoured by the gracious presence of

HER MAJESTY THE QUEEN,

Their Royal Highnesses the

Prince and Princess of Wales, Princess Louise, Princess Beatrice, &c., &c.

Few among all those who profess to know everything about Maudle and Postlethwaite, who laughed at *The Colonel* and *Patience*, can honestly say they knew anything about Aestheticism before it was made the target of our sneering satirists. The secret of the situation and the reason why it is profitable, lies in the fact that Aesthetes are supposed to belong to the "Upper Crust." One of the characteristics of the lower middle classes is an intense desire to know, or to profess to know, all that goes on in aristocratic circles. A good thing it is for our national reputation that our English comic writing and English comic draughtsmanship have a history beyond the only that can be found for them in the latter part of the nineteenth century, else these things would be merely comic by means of their audacious pretences upon comicality. As it is, even this sort of literary and artistic ware has its imitators. The only thing which reconciles one to *Punch* is, that one can generally understand his aims if one cannot always respect his motives. Very different is it with the inferior article. Providence alone knows what is meant by either type of wood blocks in two other so-called comic papers, which are never in the least comic unless unintentionally, as when they attempt to prophecy before they know.

One of these professes to be a staunch Tory journal; the other is as decidedly Liberal. Yet both are owned by *one and the same firm*, and what is still more curious is, that at time these two *politically antagonistic* organs have been edited by one and the same editor. So much for the political consistency of our comic journals.

MR. OSCAR WILDE

IT is seldom, indeed, that so very young a man as Mr. Oscar Wilde comes so prominently into public notice, and it would be neither truthful nor complimentary to ascribe the notoriety he has obtained entirely to his own exertions. Nothing can excuse the gross personal abuse which some journals, but more particularly *Punch*, have showered on him. Mr. Oscar Wilde is a gentleman by birth, education, manners, and appearance; it would be difficult to say the same of some of his opponents, and though every attack upon him is, in reality, an advertisement of his lectures and poems, that is not the motive which actuates, nor it it an excuse for, the libels and gross misrepresentations printed every day about him. The ridicule that has been lavished on his actions and dress is as unreasonable, as the excessive adulation which his poems have earned from some of the more intense Aesthetes, who look upon him as the exponent of their most extreme ideas.

Mr. Oscar O'Flahertie Wills Wilde is an Irishman by birth. His father, the late Sir William R. Wilde, was an eminent surgeon, who practised for many years in Merrion Square, Dublin. Sir William Wilde, who was born about 1815, made a special study of opthalmic and aural diseases, in which branches of his profession he was recognised as a high authority, and was appointed surgeon-ocultist to the Queen in 1853.

He was thrice appointed census commissioner for Ireland, and for his exertions in that capacity he received the honour of knighthood from the Lord-Lieutenant of Ireland, in 1864.

He was, also, distinguished as a man of literary tastes and

great archaeological learning; besides some medical works, he wrote "The Beauties of the Boyne;" a lecture entitled "Ireland, Past and Present; the Land and the People," and an account of the closing years of Jonathan Swift, Dean of St. Patrick's, Dublin; but his principal work was "A Catalogue of the Antiquities in the Royal Irish Academy," a scholarly description of the rare and curious exhibits belonging to that learned society, of which he was elected president.

In 1851 Sir William (then Mr.) Wilde married Jane Francesca Elgee, a grand daughter of Archdeacon Elgee, of Wexford, a lady well known in literary circles in Dublin, having written many poems which were published in the *Nation* newspaper at the time of the political excitement in 1848. They appeared over the *nom de plume* "Speranza," and were, of course, in favour of that Irish National cause, which even yet claims attention, and must, sooner or later, receive full and fair consideration (which it never has had) from British statesmen, or end in a civil war, and a calamitous result for either England or Ireland.

Lady Wilde's poems were afterwards published in a collected form, entitled, "Poems by Speranza," and had for a motto - "Fidanza, Speranza, Costanza." This volume, published by Cameron and Ferguson, of Glasgow, contained a portrait of Lady Wilde, and was dedicated to Ireland. In it are numerous short poems on the state of that country. One of these was on "The Brothers, Henry and John Shears, who were executed in 1798," containing the verse :-

"Yet none spring forth their bonds to sever,
Ah! methinks, had I been there,
I'd have dared a thousand deaths ere ever

The sword should touch their hair."[8]

The famine, the depopulation, and British mis-government are also alluded to, with a poem to Daniel O'Connell, and another to William Carleton, the author, who died in 1869. The second part of the volume is made up principally of translations.

In 1863 Lady Wilde produced a translation of a curious and powerful German romance, entitled "The First Temptation, or Eritis Sicut Deus." This is one of the finest works of modern German fiction, and possesses great metaphysical power. The hero is an Hegelian Philosopher, whose religion is the cultus of Beauty, and perhaps the English publisher may have feared that such a theory would shock the faith or morals of his readers, but in any case nearly the whole edition was burnt, accidentally as was supposed, and the work is now very scarce in consequence. She has also made numerous translations from the works of Alexander Dumas, Lamartine, and others, besides contributions in prose and poetry to various London magazines.

Lady Wilde has for some time past resided in London, with her son, William Charles Kingsbury Wilde, M. A., whose magazine poems have also attracted some attention.

Oscar Wilde was born in Dublin, on the 15th October, 1856, so that he is now twenty-six years of age, but brief as has been his career, it has been full of promise for the future. The son of highly intellectual parents, he has had an exceptional education,

---

[8] This was no idle boast; for Lady Wilde gave proof of her highmindedness in "Forty-Eight," when standing up in the gallery of the court, she proclaimed herself, before the judges of the Land, the author of an article which was then adduced as proof of the guilt of the editor of one of the National papers.

has travelled much in wild and remote, though classic lands, and in the course of these journeys has learnt to appreciate the beauties of the old authors, in whose works whilst at college he attained exceptional proficiency. But his naturally enthusiastic temperament teaches him to hope for better in the future than has been achieved in the past, and to see how vast will be the influence of Art and Literature on the coming democracy of Intellect, when education and culture shall have taught men to pride themselves on what they have done, and not alone on the deeds of their ancestors. Having spent about a year at Portora Royal School, Enniskillen (the Eton of Ireland), and before going to Oxford, Mr. O. Wilde studied for a year at Trinity College, in his native city, where he obtained a classical scholarship at the unusually early age of 16, and in the following year, 1874, won the Berkeley Gold Medal for Greek, the special topic selected for that year being the Greek Comic Poets. Thence he went to Magdalen College, Oxford, where he also obtained a first scholarship.

During a vacation ramble in 1877 he started for Greece, visiting Ravenna by chance on the way, he obtained material for a poem on that ancient city, and singularly enough "Ravenna" was afterwards given out as the topic for the Newdigate competition, and on the 26th June, 1878, the Newdigate prize poem, "Ravenna," by Oscar Wilde, of Magdalen, was recited in the theatre, Oxford.

> "O lone Ravenna! many a tale is told
> Of thy great glories in the days of old:
> Two thousand years have passed since thou did'st see
> Caesar ride forth to royal victory.
> Mighty thy name when Rome's lean eagles flew

From Britain's isles to far Euphrates blue;
And of the peoples thou was noble queen,
Till in thy streets the Goth and Hun were seen.
Discrowned by man, deserted by the sea,
Thou sleepest, rocked in lonely misery!
No longer now upon the swelling tide,
Pine-forest like, thy myriad galleys ride!
For where the brass-peaked ships were wont to float,
The weary shepherd pipes his mournful note;
And the white sheep are free to come and go
Where Adria's purple waters used to flow.

O fair! O sad! O queen uncomforted!
In ruined loveliness thou liest dead,
Alone of all thy sisters; for at last
Italia's royal warrior hath passed
Rome's lordliest entrance, and hath worn his crown
In the high temples of the Eternal Town!
The Palatine hath welcomed back her king,
And with his name the seven mountains ring!

And Naples hath outlived her dream of pain,
And mocks her tyrant! Venice lives again,
New risen from the waters! and the cry
Of Light and Truth, of Love and Liberty,
Is heard in lordly Genoa, and where
The marble spires of Milan wound the air,
Rings from the Alps to the Sicilian shore,
And Dante's dream is now a dream no more.

But thou, Ravenna, better loved than all,
Thy ruined palaces are but a pall

That hides thy fallen greatness! and thy name
Burns like a grey and flickering candle flame,
Beneath the noonday splendour of the sun
Of New Italia!"

This poem has since been published by T. Shrimpton and Son, Oxford, with a dedication -

"To my friend,
George Fleming,
Author of 'The Nile Novel,' and 'Mirage.' "

Whilst at Oxford, Mr. Wilde attended Mr. Ruskin's lectures on Florentine Art, and even followed that eccentric master's teaching and example by working at road-making, so that the body might be strengthened as well as the mind. But, unfortunately, Mr. Ruskin left for Venice at the end of Mr. Wilde's first term, not, however, before he had inoculated a number of the young collegians with artistic tastes. Mr. Wilde occupied some fine old wainscoted rooms over the river in that college which is thought by many to be the most beautiful in Oxford. These rooms he had decorated with painted ceilings and handsome dados, and they were filled with treasures of art, picked up at home and abroad, and here he held social meetings, which were attended by numbers of the men who were interested in art, or music, or poetry, and who for the most part practised some one of these in addition to the ordinary collegiate studies.

One who was then acquainted with Mr. O. Wilde has thus described his life at Oxford :-

"He soon began to show his taste for art and china, and before he had been at Oxford very long, his rooms were quite the show ones of the college, and of the university too. He was fortunate enough to obtain the best situated rooms in the college, on what is called the kitchen staircase, having a lovely view over the River Cherwell and the beautiful Magdalen walks and Magdalen bridge. His rooms were three in number, and the walls were entirely panelled. The two sitting rooms were connected by an arch, where folding doors had at one time stood. His blue china was supposed by connoisseurs to be very valuable and fine, and there was plenty of it. The panelled walls were thickly hung with old engravings - chiefly engravings of the fair sex artistically clad as nature clad them. He was hospitable, and on Sunday nights after 'Common Room,' his rooms were generally the scene of conviviality, where undergraduates of all descriptions and tastes were to be met, drinking punch, or a B. and S. with their cigars. It was at one of these entertainments that he made his well-known remark, 'Oh, would that I could live up to my blue china!' His chief amusement was riding, though he never used to hunt. He was generally to be met on the cricket field, but never played himself, and he was a regular attendant at his college barge to see the May eight-oar races, but he never used to trust his massive form to a boat himself."

With all this, he managed to take a first in classical moderations in Trinity term, 1876, though he was seldom seen reading. After this he spent some months travelling in Greece and Palestine. Besides minor scholarships, he took the Newdigate, a prize for English verse, in 1878, and in June of the same year, he took a first in *Literis Humanioribus*, after which he took his degree.

During this period he produced a number of poems, some of them the outcome of his visits to Italy, and full of the fervour of Roman Catholicism, which the glories of art as shown in the gorgeous temples of that religion are sure to create in the breasts of its votaries when first they visit Florence, Rome, or Milan.

These were published, some in *The Month*, others in the *Catholic Monitor*, and the *Irish Monthly*. A number of short poems also appeared in *Kottabos*, a small magazine written by members of Trinity College, Dublin. Most of these have since been republished in his volume of poems, thus the *Ballade de Marguerite* originally appeared in *Kottabos*, for 1879, as

"LA BELLE MARGUERITE."
Ballade du Moyen Age

"I am weary of lying within the chase,
While the knyghtes are meeting in market place.

Nay, go not thou to the red-roof'd town,
Lest the hooves of the war-horse tread thee down.

But I would not go where the squires ride;
I would only sit by my lady's side.

Alack! and alack! thou are over bold,
A forester's son may not eat off of gold.

Will she love me less, that my father is seen
Each Martinmas Dy in a doublet green?

But your cloak of sheepskin is rough to see,
When your lady is clad in cramoisie.

Alack! and alack! them, if true love dies,
When one is in silk, and the other in frieze!

Mayhap she is working the tapestrie;
Spindle and loom are not meet for thee.

If it be that she seweth the arras bright,
I might ravel the threads by the fire light.

Mayhap she is chasing of the deer;
How could you follow o'er hill and meer?

If it be that she hunteth with the Court,
I might run behind her, and wind the mort

Mayhap she is praying in chapellrie
(To her soul may our Lady show gramercie!)

Ah! if she is kneeling in lone chapélle,
I might swing the censer, or ring the bell.

Come in, my son, for thou look'st sae pale
Thy father will fill thee a stoup of ale.

Oh! who are these knyghtes in bright array?
Is it a pageant the rich folk play?

It's the King of France from over the sea,
That has come to visit our fair countrie.

But why does the curfew toll sae low?
And why do the mourners walk a-row?

Oh, it's Hugh of Durham, my sister's son,
That is lying stark, for his day is done.

Ah, no, for I se white lilies clear;
It is no strong man that lies on the bier.

Oh! it's good Dame Alice that kept the Hall:
I knew she would die at the autumn fall.

Dame Alice was not a maiden fair,
Dame Alice had not that yellow hair.

Oh, it's none of our kith and none of our kin;
(Her soul may Our Lady assoil from sin).

But I hear the boy's voice chanting sweet,
'Elle est morte, la Marguerite!'

Come in, my son, and lie on the bed,
And let the dead folk bury their dead.

Oh! mother, you know I loved her true:
Oh, mother, one grave will do for two."

———————————

The first number of Edmund Yates' Magazine, *Time*, appeared in April, 1879; this contained a short poem by Oscar Wilde, appropriately entitled, "The Conqueror of Time," and in the July part of the same year there was another, and most exquisite melody, "The New Helen." Some of the foregoing, with others not previously published, appeared in an elegant volume issued by David Bogue, in 1881, entitled, "Poems" by Oscar Wilde. Now, at the time these poems were published, Mr. Burnand's play, *The Colonel*, had recently been brought out, and he was able at once to puff his own production and to ridicule that of Mr. Wilde in his journal. The review of the Poems contained in *Punch* commenced thus :-

"Mr. Lambert Streyke, in *The Colonel*, published a book of poems for the benefit of his followers and his own; Mr. Oscar Wilde has followed his example."

In order to appreciate the exquisite taste and delicate satire of this sentence, we have only to bear in mind that the character of Lambert Streyke in the play is that of a paltry swindler, who, shamming Aesthetic tastes, imposes upon a number of rather silly ladies an is finally exposed by the Colonel. The par, in fact, is that of a mere pitiful humbug, whose art is a sham, and his conversation and manners ridiculous and outrageous exaggerations of those of even the most extreme Aesthete.

Following up this comparison of Mr. Oscar Wilde to a shallow swindler, *Punch's* amiable critic goes on to observe :-

"The cover is consummate, the paper is distinctly precious, the binding is beautiful, and the type is utterly too.

"*Poems, by Oscar Wilde*, that is the title of the book of the Aesthetic singer, which comes to us arrayed in white vellum and gold. There is a certain amount of originality about the binding, but that is more than can be said for the inside of the volume. Mr. Wilde may be Aesthetic, but he is not original. This is a volume of echoes, it is Swinburne and water while here and there we note that the author has been reminiscent of Mr. Rossetti and Mrs. Browning.

"To sum up, these outpourings of our Aesthetic bard must be pronounced poor and pretentious stuff."

Now I have no intention of comparing Mr. Wilde with any of our greater poets, but I do wish to call attention to the fact that he is still a very young man; the early works of Shelley, Keats, Byron and Tennyson, were pronounced by the critics, also, to be "poor and pretentious stuff," so Mr. Wilde need not be greatly disturbed by these spiteful criticisms, especially as his poems have already run through four editions.

When Christopher North slashed into Tennyson's first volume, the future poet-laureate scribbled a few contemptuous verses in reply; the lines might, with a very slight alteration, be used by Oscar Wilde.

"You did late review my lays,
Crusty Charivari;

142

You did mingle blame and praise,
        Rusty Charivari.
When I learnt from whom it came
        I forgave you all the blame,
I could *not* forgive the praise,
        Fusty Charivari."

As, however, I have his volume before me, I will select a few extracts from it, which will enable a reader to form his own judgement, unbiased by *Punch's* spiteful comments :-

"RESQUIESCAT.

Tread lightly, she is near,
        Under the snow,
Speak gently, she can hear
        The daisies grow.

All her bright golden hair
        Tarnished with rust,
She that was young and fair,
        Fallen to dust.

Lily-like, white as snow,
        She hardly knew
She was a woman, so
        Sweetly she grew.

Coffin board, heavy stone,
        Lie on her breast,
I vex my heart alone,
        She is at rest.

Peace, peace, she cannot hear
        Lyre or sonnet,

All my life's buried here,

Heap earth upon it."

Is there anything sweeter or more pathetic in Tom Hood than these few lines? I think not.

Here is another in a similar vein of pathos :-

"IMPRESSION DU MATIN.

The Thames nocturne in blue and gold
Changed to a harmony in gray:
A barge with ochre-coloured hay
Dropt from the wharf; and chill and cold.

The yellow fog came creeping down
The bridges, till the houses' walls
Seemed changed to shadows, and St. Paul's
Loomed like a bubble o'er the town.

Then suddenly arose the clang
Of waking life; the streets were stirred
With country wagons: and a bird
Flew to the glistening roofs and sang.

But one pale woman all alone,
The daylight kissing her wan hair,
Loitered beneath the gas-lamp's flare,
With lips of flame and heart of stone."

The longest poem in the volume tells how *Charmides* obtained access into the sacred secret temple of Minerva, and the terrible vengeance the haughty virgin goddess took upon him, and the maid who he loved. This poem abounds with both the merits and the faults of Mr. Oscar Wilde's style - it is classical, sad, voluptuous, and full of passages of the most exquisitely musical word painting; but it is cloying from its very sweetness - the elaboration of its details makes it over luscious. It is no mere trick to be able to write thus; it betrays a luxuriant fancy and a great command of language; youth is apt to be exuberant, age will mellow down his muse, and then Mr. Wilde's undoubted genius will produce something finer even than *Charmides*.

Poets do not at all times express their own individual opinions in their works, nor it is advisable they should; theirs it is to portray many minds, and many moods of many men; yet, without doubt, the ideas expressed in "Ave Imperatrix" are those of Mr. Wilde, and they show him to be a Republican, not of the noisy and blatant, but of the quiet and patient kind, content to wait till the general spread of democracy, and the absorption of governing power by the people, shall peacefully bring about the changes they desire, and remove the abuses of our present *régime*.

"AVE IMPERATRIX.

"Set in this stormy Northern sea,
　　Queen of these restless fields of tide,
England! what shall men say of thee,
　　Before whose feet the worlds divide?

For southern wind and east wind meet
　　Where, girt and crowned by sword and fire,
England with bare and bloody feet
　　Climbs the steep road of wide empire.

Here have our wild war eagles flown,
　　And flapped wide wings in fiery fight;
But the sad dove, that sits alone
　　In England - she hath no delight.

In vain the laughing girl will lean
    To greet her love with love-lit eyes:
Down in some treacherous black ravine,
    Clutching his flag, the dead boy lies.

And many a moon and sun will see
    The lingering wistful children wait
To climb upon their father's knee;
    And in each house made desolate

Pale women who have lost their lord
    Will kiss the relics of the slain -
Some tarnished epaulette - some sword -
    Poor toys to soothe such anguished pain

For not in quiet English fields
    Are these, our brothers, lain to rest
Where we might deck their broken shields
    With all the flowers the dead love best.

For some are by the Delhi walls,
    And many in the Afghan land,
And many where the Ganges falls
    Through seven mouths of shifting sand.

And some in Russian waters lie,
    And others in the seas which are
The portals to the East, or by
    The wind-swept heights of Trafalgar.

O wandering graves! O restless sleep!
    O silence of the sunless day!
O still ravine! O stormy deep!
    Give up your prey! give up your prey!

146

And thou whose wounds are never healed
    Whose weary race is never won,
O Cromwell's England! must thou yield
    For every inch of ground a son?

Go! crown with thorns thy gold-crowned head,
    Change thy glad song to song of pain;
Wind and wild wave have got thy dead,
    And will not yield them back again.

Where are the brave, the strong, the fleet?
    Where is our English chivalry?
Wild grasses are their burial sheet,
    And sobbing waves their threnody.

O loved ones lying far away,
    What word of love can dead lips send!
O wasted dust! O senseless clay!
    Is this the end? is this the end?

Peace, peace! we wrong the noble dead
    To vex their solemn slumber so;
Though childless, and with thorn-crowned head,
    Up the steep road must England go.

Yet when this fiery web is spun,
    Her watchman shall descry from far,
The young Republic, like a sun,
    Rise from these crimson seas of war."

But those who would find the true ring of Aesthetic poetry, must indeed go to the book itself; even a Philistine may find delight in its perusal, if *he will*; or if he prefer to scoff and jibe so let it be. For such a one nothing but pity should be felt -

for truly the gift of appreciating the beautiful in nature, or in art, is not given to every man, and he who has it not is as one who is colour-blind; he is sense-blind, or sound-blind, and deserves commiseration.

In addition to poetry, Mr. Wilde has written various prose articles, amongst them one on Keats, and a critique on the Grosvenor Gallery of 1877, an introduction to the poems of Rennell Rodd,[9] also a drama, entitled "Nora, or the Nihilist." This play has no yet been produced, probably because of the powerful situations it contains founded on democratic ideas. Such a play would be more likely to find acceptance in the States, where the censorship of the drama is *not* confided to n amiable old gentleman attached to the household of the Royal Family, connected by marriage with all the depots in Europe - of whom one or two might possibly take offence at Mr. Wilde's outspoken denunciations of their tyranny and oppression.

One of the first principles of Aestheticism is that all the fine arts are intimately related to one another; hence we see that their poets have been painters, whilst their artists have largely availed themselves of the creations of the poets as topics for their principal pictures and statues.

---

[9] *Rose Leaf and Apple Leaf,* by Rennell Rodd, with an introduction by Oscar Wilde (Philadelphia: J. M. Stoddart & Co. 1882). A dainty little volume of poems clothed in most exquisite attire. The printed matter occupies one side only of a thin transparent sheet of hand-made parchment paper, interleaved with pale apple green, the delicate tint of which shows through the printed page in a manner most grateful to the readers' eyes. The illustrations are of a decidedly Japanese type, and the outer case is of white vellum. Oscar Wilde's introduction (though written prose) reads like a poem in praise of a poem, for his language is rich and musical, though perhaps his style may be thought a trifle involved.

Having dealt with the *poems* of Mr. Wilde, it is now necessary to refer to his career in the two other capacities he has assumed of *Art Lecturer* and *Dress Reformer*, in both of which characters he has perhaps earned wider and more general celebrity than in that of poet.

As the original of Archibald Grosvenor in *Patience*, he could well afford to smile at the good-humoured satire of Mr. Gilbert's sketch, which assuredly has no malice in it. But the ill-natured and grossly-personal attacks of *Punch*, in which he figured so long as Jellaby Postlethwaite, are far less laughable, whilst the spite they embodied was carefully reproduced in *The Colonel*, where the character of Lambert Streyke is shown as the epitome of humbug, vulgarity, and hypocrisy; the chief difference being that whereas it was generally understood that skits on J. P. in *Punch* were levelled at Oscar Wilde, the character of Lambert Streyke in *The Colonel* was made so base and revolting that although some of Du Maurier's stale old jokes about Postlethwaite were reproduced, no one would venture to connect Streyke with Oscar Wilde. Yet one cannot forget that the author, or rather the *adapter*, of *The Colonel* was also the Editor of *Punch*, and that Du Maurier satirized the new School of Aesthetes before Burnand compiled *The Colonel*, from various sources with which reading people have long been only too familiar.

No doubt some of the popular ridicule of the Aesthetic School has been brought about by Mr. Oscar Wilde, whose peculiarities of garb have been seized upon by sapient critics, who find it easier to laugh at his knee breeches than his poetry, which for the greater part they appear not to have read.

A very general opinion about the school appears to be that it is "a mutual admiration society, artificially heated by the steam of reciprocal incense for the incubation of coterie glory"; to somewhat dispel that illusion I have already enumerated some of the principal men connected with it, and finding such names as Ruskin, Swinburne, the Rossettis, Morris, and E. Burne-Jones, besides numerous artists who are enthusiastic in the support of the ethics of the school, it is surely time the public should form an opinion of their own, and no longer take their ideas at second-hand from a played-out would-be comic journal.

They should at least bear in mind the good that has been effected by the movement, whose effects they see around them in the vast improvements recently made in furniture, and house decoration, and other branches of art.

The interest in the Aesthetic School had sometime since spread to the United States, where the cheap reprints of the works of our most famous authors quickly procure as wide a circle of readers as they can obtain in this country. Hence, when the opera of *Patience* was produced, its points were fully appreciated by *reading* people; and it occurred to Mr. Wilde that a visit to the States to give some lectures, explanatory of *real Aestheticism* as it exists amongst us, might interest and possibly instruct and elevate our rich and clever, if not particularly *cultured* transatlantic cousins.

In some of his early utterances he was unguarded; he admitted, for instance, that he was not greatly impressed with the mighty ocean. Here was a splendid opportunity for the comic journals, great was the flow of wit from this small cause :-

"There's *Oscar Wilde*, that gifted chylde,
Fair Poesie's anointed,
Has, like a brick, the Atlantic
Crossed, to be disappointed.
Poor Oscar Wilde, aesthetic chylde;

The Atlantic ought to know it

A fault so grave to misbehave,

And disappoint a poet!"

Such is American newspaper enterprise, that before Oscar Wilde could set his foot on shore he was interviewed, and thoroughly cross-examined; I may as well quote one of the descriptions: it will serve as a sample of the kind of writing that goes down in the Unites States :-

" 'Men may come and men may go,' says the scribe of the *New York Herald*, 'but it is not every day that an apostle (thwaite) of aestheticism comes to the shores of America. It was for this reason that the *Herald* reporter met Mr. Oscar Wilde at the first available place - namely, quarantine.'

"Mr. Wilde 'was not at all adverse to the American process of interviewing,' and began by informing the reporter that he had come to the United States 'to lecture on the Renaissance,' which he defined as the 'revival of the intimate study of the correlation of all arts.'

" 'I shall lecture,' said Mr. Wilde, a little reservedly, 'in Chickering Hall on the Renaissance. My future movements will depend entirely upon the results of my lecture in a business sense. I have come here with the intention of producing upon an American stage a play which I have written, and which I have not, for reasons, been able to produce in London. It is exceedingly desirable that it should be produced with a cast of actors who shall be thoroughly able to represent the piece with all the force of its original conception.'

" 'But,' said the reporter, 'do you not intend to produce a volume of poems while you are in America?'

" 'No, I shall not, certainly for some time to come, publish another volume; but I hardly care to say what the future may develop.'

" 'You will certainly lecture, however?' said the reporter.

" 'I certainly shall, but I do not know whether I shall lecture in other cities besides New York. It will depend entirely upon what encouragement I find in the acceptance of my school of philosophy.'

" 'Do you then call "aestheticism" a philosophy?' asked the reporter.

" 'Most certainly it is a philosophy. It is the study of what may be found in art. It is the pursuit of the secret of life. Whatever there is in all art that represents the eternal truth, is an expression of the great underlying truth. So far aestheticism may be held to be the study of truth in art.'

" 'Aestheticism,' said the reporter, 'has been understood in America to be a blind groping after something which is entirely intangible. Can you, as the exponent of aestheticism, give an interpretation which shall serve to give a more respectable standing to the word?'

" 'I do not know,' said Mr. Wilde, 'that I have give a much better definition that I have already given. But whatever there has been in poetry since the time of Keats, whatever there has been in art that has served to devolve the underlying principles of truth; whatever there has been in science that has served to show the individual meaning of truth as expressed to humanity - that has been an exponent of aestheticism.'

The most amusing of all the paragraphs that have appeared in *Punch* about Oscar Wilde, was the burlesque description of

"Oscar Interviewed.

"New York, Jan, 1882.

"Determined to anticipate the rabble of penny-a-liners to

pounce upon any distinguished foreigner who approaches our shores, and eager to assist a sensitive Poet in avoiding the impertinent curiosity and ill-bred insolence of the Professional Reporter, I took the fastest pilot-boat on the station, and boarded the splendid Cunard steamer, *The Bostonia*, in the shucking of a pea-nut.

"HIS AESTHETIC APPEARANCE.

"He stood, with his large hand passed through his long hair, against a high chimney-piece - which had been painted pea-green, with panels of peacock-blue pottery let in at uneven intervals - one elbow on the high ledge, the other hand on his hip. He was dressed in a long, snuff-coloured, single-breasted coat, which reached to his heels, and was relieved with a seal-skin collar and cuffs rather the worse for wear. Frayed linen, and an orange silk handkerchief gave a note to the generally artistic colouring of the *ensemble*, while one small daisy drooped despondently in his button-hole. . . . We may state, that the chimney-piece, as well as the sealskin collar, is the property of Oscar, and will appear in his lectures 'on the Growth of Artistic Taste in England.' But

"HE SPEAKS FOR HIMSELF.

" 'Yes; I should have been astonished had I not been interviewed! Indeed I have not been well on board this Cunard Argosy. I have wrestled with the glaukous-haired Poseidon and feared his ravishment. Quite: I have been too ill, too utterly ill. Exactly - seasick, in fact, if I must descend to so trivial an expression. I fear the clean beauty of my strong limbs is somewhat waned. I am scarcely myself - my nerves are thrilling like throbbing violins, in exquisite pulsation.

"You are right. I believe I was the first to devote my subtle brain-chords to the worship of the sunflower, and the apotheosis of the delicate Tea-pot. I have ever been jasmine-cradled from my youth. Eons ago, I might say centuries, in '78, when a student at Oxford, I had trampled the vintage of my babyhood, and trod the thorn-spread heights of Poesy. I had stood in the Arena and torn the bays from the expiring athletes, my competitors."

"HIS GLORIOUS PAST.

"Precisely - I took the Newdigate. Oh! no doubt, every year some man gets the Newdigate; but not every year does Newdigate get an Oscar. Since then - barely three years, but centuries to such as I am - I have stood upon the steps of London Palaces - in South Kensington - and preached Aesthetic art. I have taught the wan beauty to wear nameless robes, have guided her limp limbs into sightless knots and curving festoons, while we sand of the sweet sad sin of Swinburne, or the lone delight of soft communion with Burne-Jones. Swinburne had made a name, and Burne-Jones had copied illuminations e'er the first silky down had fringed my upper lip, but the Trinity of Inner Brotherhood was not complete till I came forward, like the Asphodel from the wilds of Arcady, to join in sweet antiphonal counterchanges with the Elder seers. We are a Beautiful Family - we are, we are, we are!"

"LECTURE PROSPECTS.

"Yes; I expect my lecture will be a success. So does Dollar Carte - I mean D'Oyly Carte. Too-Toothless Senility may jeer, and poor positive Propriety may shake her rusty curls; but I am here, in my creamy lustihood, to pipe of Passion's venturous Poesy, and reap the scorching harvest of Self-Love! I am not quite sure hat I mean. The true Poet never is. In fact, true Poetry is nothing if it is intelligible. She is only to be compared to Salmacis, who is not boy or girl, but yet is both."

"HIS NEOPHYTES.

"Who are my neophytes! Well, I fancy the Lonsdales and Langtrys would have never been known if I hadn't placed them on a pedestal of daffodils, and taught the world to worship."

"HIS KOSMIC SOUL.

"Oh, yes! I speak most languages; in the sweet honey-tinted brogue my own land lends me. *La bella Donna della mia Mente* exists, but she is not the Jersey Lily, though I have grovelled at her feel; she is not the Juno Countess, though I have twisted my limbs all over her sofas; she is not the Polish Actress, though I have sighed and wept over all the boxes of the Court Theatre; she is not the diaphanous Sarah, though I have crawled after her footsteps through the heavy fields of scentless Asphodel; she is not the golden haired Ellen, more fair than any woman Veronesé looked upon, though I have left my *Impressions* on many and many a seat in the Lyceum Temple, where she is High Priestess; nor is she one of the little Nameless Naiads I have met in Lotus-haunts, who, with longing eyes, watch the sweet bubble of the frenzied grape. No, Sir, my real Love is my own Kosmic Soul, enthroned in its flawless essence; and when America can grasp the supreme whole I sing in too-too utterance for vulgar lips, them my soul and body will blend in mystic symphonies; then, crowned with bellamours and wanton flower-de-luce, I shall be hailed Lord of a new Empery, and as I stain my lips in the bleeding wounds of the Pomegranate, and wreathe my o'ergrown limbs with the burnished disk of the Sun, the tamer chariot of a forgotten god will make way for the glorious zenith of the one Oscar Wilde."

The next report I shall quote gives an account of Mr. Wilde's first lecture in New York, in which he went very fully into the whole question of modern art. The New York World gave an excellent précis of his utterances on that occasion, which is worthy of quotation, as containing one of the best expositions of the aims of the Aesthetic School :-

"It is seldom that Chickering Hall has contained so fine an audience as that which gathered there last evening to see Mr. Oscar Wilde, and to listen to his exposition of those peculiar views which have distinguished him from everyday folk in England. And Mr. Wilde was well worth seeing, his short breeches and silk stockings showing to even better advantage upon the stage than in the gilded drawing-rooms, where the young apostle has heretofore been seen in New York. No sunflower, nor yet a lily, dangled from the button-hole of his coat; indeed, there is room for reasonable doubt as to whether his coat had even one button-hole to be put to such artistic use. But judging his coat by the laws of the Philistines, it was a well-fitting coat, and looked as though it had been made for the wearer as a real coat, and not as a mere piece of decorative drapery. Promptly at 8 o'clock the young lecturer came upon the stage, and with the briefest possible introduction from Colonel Morse, Mr. Wilde began his lecture.

"A subject as evasive as beauty, for beauty was the real subject of the lecture, is difficult to grasp with logic. Not analysis, not descriptive was the method of treatment, but revelation. 'Beauty cannot be taught, but only revealed,' is the apothegm that Mr. Wilde never tires of repeating; and this, fitly enough, is the key to his style. He handled no prosaic subject, nor was his handling prosaic. Long melodious sentences, seldom involved, always clear, unfolded his meaning, as graceful curves reveal a beautiful figure. A vocabulary as wide as Swinburne's and well-nigh as musical, modelled on that rich and flowing prose, which is as marvellous as Swinburne's verse - how could such a style be dull? Yet it was never obscure. Always the first clear principle of chaste English, simplicity, and the careful attribute of clean thought, exactness, characterised his style. Almost gorgeous at times, his language never quite ran away with him, but was always equal to the clear expression of the most subtle fancy. The best parts of the lecture were its clear glimpses of a rare appreciation of artistic literary work from Homer to William Morris. It is not every day that one can sit in the hearing of so keen a critic, or catch such glimpses of so clear a revelation of art. Perhaps the young poet may yet lack strength, but he certainly does not lack fluency, width, and felicity of style.

"Among the many debts, said Mr. Oscar Wilde, which we owe to the supreme aesthetic faculty of Goethe is that he was the first to teach us to define beauty in terms the most concrete possible; to realise it, I mean, always in its special manifestations. So, in the lecture which I have the honour to deliver before you, I will not try to give you any abstract definition of beauty, any such universal formula for it as was sought by the philosophy of the eighteenth century; still less to communicate to you that which in its essence is incommunicable - the virtue by which a particular picture or poem affects us with a unique and special joy, but rather to point out to you the general ideas which characterise the great English renaissance of art in this century. The renaissance

157

has been described as a mere revival of Greek modes of thought; and again as a mere revival of mediaeval feeling. It is really from the union of Hellenism in its breadth; its sanity of purpose; its calm possession of beauty, with the intensified individualism, the passionate colours of the romantic spirit that springs the art of the nineteenth century in England, as from the marriage of Faust and Helen of Troy sprang the beautiful boy Euphorion. I trace the first tendencies of the modern renaissance to the French Revolution, and the desire for perfection which lay at the base of that revolution found in a young English poet its most complete and flawless realisation. Phidias and the achievements of Greek art are foreshadowed in Homer; Dante prefigures for us the passion and colour and intensity of Italian painting; the modern love of landscape dates from Rousseau; and it is in Keats that one discerns the beginning of the artistic renaissance of England. Byron was a rebel, and Shelley a dreamer; but in the calmness and clearness of his vision, his self-control, his unerring sense of beauty, and his recognition of a separate realm for the imagination, Keats was the pure and serene artist, the forerunner of the Pre-Raphaelite School, and so of the great romantic movement of which I am to speak.

"If you ask nine-tenths of the British public about the Pre-Raphaelites, you will hear something about an eccentric lot of young men to whom belong a sort of divine crookedness and holy awkwardness in drawing all the chief objects of art. To know nothing about their great men is one of the necessary elements of English education. Indeed, the average Englishman will tell you that aestheticism is the French for affectation, or the German for dado. The Pre-Raphaelites were a number of young poets and painters who banded together in London about thirty years since to revolutionize English poetry and painting. They had three things which the English public never forgive - youth, power, and enthusiasm. Satire paid them the homage which mediocrity pays to genius. Their detractors blinded the public, but simply confirmed the artists in their convictions. To disagree with three-fourths of all England on all points is one of the first elements of sanity.

"Pre-Raphaelism was above all things a return to nature - to draw and paint nothing but what was seen. With the joining of William Morris and Edward Burne-Jones to the original board came changes. The latter brought to painting a more exquisite choice, a more faultless devotion to beauty, a more intense seeking after perfection. He felt that the close imitation of nature was a disturbing element in imaginative art. To Morris we owe poetry whose perfect precision and clearness of word and vision have not been excelled in the literature of our country. This revolution was not only one of ideas, but of creations. The poetry of Morris, Swinburne, and Rossetti shows a style flawless and fearless, a sustaining consciousness of the musical value of each word, a distinct advance in technique, which is the characteristic of all great eras.

"While then, the material for workmanship is being elaborated, what people call the poet's inspiration has not escaped the controlling influence of the artistic spirit; not that the imagination has lost its wings, but we have accustomed ourselves to count their innumerable pulsations, to estimate their limitless strength, to govern their ungovernable freedom.

"In choosing his subject, the artist is the spectator of all time. Past and present are alike real to him. For him no form is obsolete, no subject out of date. But all things are not fit subjects for poetry. Into the sacred house of Beauty the true artist will admit nothing which is harsh or disturbing, nothing about which men argue. If he writes on these subjects, he does do, as Milton expresses it, with his left hand.

"Whatever spiritual message an artist brings to his age is matter for his own soul. It is for us to do naught but accept his teaching. But our restless modern intellectual spirit is not receptive enough. Only a few have learned the secret of those high hours when thought is not. The secret of the influence of Japanese art here in the West is that it has kept true to its primary and poetical conditions, and has not had laid on it the burden of its own intellectual doubts, the spiritual tragedy of its own sorrows. In its primary aspect a painting has no more spiritual message than an exquisite fragment of Venetian glass. It is a certain inventive and creative handling of line and colour which touches the soul - something entirely independent of anything poetical in the subject - something satisfying in itself. And in poetry the pleasure comes from what Keats calls the sensual life of verse, an inventive handling of rhythmical language.

"And criticism - what place is that to have in our culture? I think the first duty of an art-critic is to hold his tongue at all times and upon all subjects, said Mr. Wilde, and then with an inconsistency not elsewhere noticed in the lecture, explained that it is the critic's place to teach the public to find in the calm of art the highest expression of their own most stormy passions. 'I have no reverence,' said Keats, 'for the public or anything in existence but the Eternal Being, the memory of great men and the Principle of Beauty.' Such, then, is the spirit which I believe to be guiding and underlying our English renaissance. But it is incomplete. There can be no great sculpture without a beautiful national life, and no drama without a noble national life. The commercial spirit of England has killed both beauty and nobility."

"The drama is the meeting-place of art and life; it is the product of a period of great united energy. It is impossible without a noble public. Shelley felt how incompetent the movement was in this direction, and has shown in one great tragedy by what terror and pity he would have purified our age. He has had no worthy imitators. You have listened to the charming music of Mr. Sullivan and the clever satire of Mr. Gilbert for 300 nights, and I am sure, having given so much time to satire, it is not asking too much to ask you to listen to the truth for one evening. There is no inordinate fondness for vegetable loves among us, though we grant the cleverness of Mr. Gilbert's satire; but such satire is no truer representation of us than the dust in a beam of light is a representation of the sun, or the bubble that bursts upon the wave is a representation of the boundless sea.

"It is rather to you that we turn to perfect what we have begun. There is something Hellenic in your air and world. You are young; 'no hungry generations tread you down,' and the past does not mock you with the ruins of a beauty, the secret of whose creation you have lost.

"Love art for its own sake, and then all things that you need will be added to you."

In February Mr. Oscar Wilde lectured at Boston, to an immense audience. It was announced beforehand that sixty Harvard students would attend, dressed in imitation of Mr. Wilde. The audience was largely attracted to this announcement, but while respectable, it contained no prominent persons. The students occupied the front seats, wearing dress coats, knee-breeches, flowing wigs, and green scarves, having lilies in their buttonholes and sunflowers in their hands. Mr. Wilde did not wear the knee-breeches. Whenever he paused to drink water the audience broke into uproarious applause lasting several minutes. This occurred so often that Mr. Wilde paused and glared upon the audience until silence was restored. His impressions of Boston are said to be unpleasant, and it must be apparent that Bostonian students have but the most rudimentary ideas of the behaviour befitting gentlemen.

The *Boston Evening Transcript*, of February 2nd, 1882, thus describes the scene :-

"Boston is certainly indebted to Oscar Wilde for one thing - the thorough-going chastening of the superabounding spirits of the Harvard freshman. It will be some time, we think, before a Boston assemblage is again invaded by a body of college youths, massed as such, to take possession of the meeting. This is not unimportant, for if the thing should grow into a practice and succeed, everything in the way of public entertainments here must finally be done with the leave only of the youngest and most ill-bred class of Harvard students. Whether in his first off-hand observations, or in the pointed remarks scattered through his address, or in the story he told of the Oxford boys and Mr. Ruskin, nothing could have been more gracious, more dignified, more gentle and sweet, and yet more crushing, than the lecturer's whole demeanour to them, and its influence upon the great audience was very striking. A goodly number of the latter, it seemed to us, had gone there to see the fun, in hopes of a jolly row; but the tide of feeling was so completely turned by Mr.

Wilde's courteous and kindly dignity that even this portion of the audience took sides with him, and hissed down every attempt on the part of the rougher element to disconcert or interrupt the speaker by exaggerated and ill-timed applause. Mr. Wilde achieved a real triumph, and it was by right of conquest, by force of being a *gentleman*, in the truest sense of the word. His nobility not only obliged *him* - it obliged his would-be mockers - to good behaviour. He crowned his triumph, and he heaped coals of fire upon those curly and wiggy heads, when he, with simplicity and evident sincerity, made them an offer of a statue of a Greek athlete to stand in their gymnasium, and said he should esteem it an honour if they would accept it. This really seemed to stun the boys, for they even forgot to recognize the offer with applause. It was a lovely, though sad sight, to see those dear silly youths go out of the Music Hall in slow procession, hanging their heads meekly, and trying to avoid observation, followed by faint expressions of favour from their friends, but also with some hisses. A lady near us said, 'How mortified I should be if a son of mine were among them!' We think that every one who witnessed the scene on Tuesday evening must feel about it very much as we do, and that those who came to scoff, if they did not exactly remain to pray, at least left the Music Hall with feelings of cordial liking, and perhaps, to their own surprise, of respect for Oscar Wilde."

Mr. Wilde appears to have borne the insults of these shallow-pated imbeciles with perfect good humour and gentlemanly composure. That the fools who planned such disgraceful proceedings were utterly ignorant of the philosophy they went to ridicule, was so obvious that to treat them with silent contempt was at once the Poet's best reply and most severe rebuke.

He went to Omaha, where, under the auspices of the Social Art Club, he delivered a lecture on "Decorative Art," in the course of which he described his impressions of many American houses as being "illy designed, decorated shabbily and in bad taste, and filled with furniture that was not honestly made and was out of character." This statement gave rise to the following verses :-

"What a shame and what a pity,
In the streets of London City
   Mr. Wilde is sen no more.
Far from Piccadilly banished,
He to Omaha has vanished,
   Horrid place, which *swells* ignore.

On his back a coat he beareth,
Such as Sir John Bennett weareth,
   Made of velvet - strange array!
Legs *Apollo* might have sighed for,
Or great *Hercules* had died for,
   Hi knee breeches now display.

Waving sunflower and lily,
He calls all the houses "illy"
   Decorated and designed.
For of taste they've not a tittle;
They may chew and they may whittle;
   But they are all born colour blind!"

Wherever he went in the States he created a sensation, and it was gravely asserted that he had been induced to cross the Atlantic in order to work up an interest in *Patience*, the *satire* of that opera not having been sufficiently understood in the States except by *reading* people. Such an idea had probably never entered his head; he is scarcely the man to condescend to become an advertising medium for a play which professes to ridicule nearly everything he holds sacred in art and poetry, but his visit did certainly have a most beneficial effect upon the success of the piece, which, beyond a certain point, had created little interest amongst middle-class Americans, whose ideas of *culture* are only awakened by an occasional visit to Europe. In this category I do not, of course, include the Harvard and Rochester students, whose good taste and perfect courtesy have all the refined dignity of the *ancienne noblesse*.

Possibly Mr. Wilde cares little for the laughter of these people, provided they pay, and in this respect his lectures have been thoroughly successful, for crowded audiences have everywhere attended them - audiences composed of the most fashionable and distinguished citizens of the States, and if they have not quite caught the spirit of the movement, or have been unable to fully appreciate the teachings of the young philosopher, the fault is theirs, and not Mr. Oscar Wilde's.

Socially, of course, he was treated after the fashion of the country where Mrs. Leo Hunters about, and at the gatherings he attended the young lady element was generally in the ascendant; young men being, not unnaturally, somewhat jealous of the attentions shown to the handsome stranger, round about whom the rapturous maidens posed and sighed.

"Oh, Mr. Wilde," said one of these fair enthusiasts, "you have been adored in New York, but in Boston you will be worshipped."

"But I do not wish to be worshipped," was Mr. Wilde's sensible and modest reply.

From the States he went to Canada, visiting Quebec, Montreal, Ottawa, Kingston, and Toronto; in the latter city he was present at a Lacrosse match between the Torontos and St. Regis Indians, which he pronounced a charming game, quite ahead of cricket in some respects. His lecture in the Grand Opera House, Toronto, was attended by 1,100 persons, and wherever he went his movements and lectures created great interest.

From Canada he went to Nova Scotia, and the Halifax *Morning Herald*, of October 10, 1882, reports his lectures on "The Decorative Arts," and "The House Beautiful," it also contains an amusing account of an interview held with him by their own "Interviewer," who says he was received with winning and polite friendliness. "The apostle had no lily, not yet a sunflower. He wore a velvet jacket which seemed to be a good jacket. He had an ordinary neck tie and wore a linen collar about number eighteen on a neck half a dozen sizes smaller. His legs were in trousers, and his boots were apparently the product of New York art, judging by their pointed toes. His hair is the color of straw, slightly leonine, and when not looked after, goes climbing all over his features. Mr. Wilde was communicative and genial; he said he found Canada pleasant, but in answer to a question as to whether European or American women were the more beautiful fe dextrously evaded his querist :- "That I cannot answer here, I shall wait till I get in mid-ocean, out of sight of both countries. Your women are pretty, especially in the south, but the prettiness is in colour and freshness and bloom, and most of your ladies will not be pretty in ten years."

"I believe you discovered Mrs. Langtry?" a look of rapture came to Oscar's face, and with a gesture, the first of the interview, he said :- "I would rather have discovered Mrs. Langtry than have discovered America. Her beauty is in outline perfectly moulded. She will be a beauty at eight-five. Yes, it was for such ladies that Troy was destroyed, and well might Troy be destroyed for such a woman." The remainder of the conversation was devoted to poetry; he expressed his opinion that Poe was the greatest American poet, and that Walt Whitman, if not a poet, is a man who sounds a strong note, perhaps neither prose nor poetry, but something of his own that is grand, original and unique.[10]

After leaving Halifax, Oscar Wilde went to lecture in several smaller towns in Nova Scotia, amongst others to Moncton, where his experiences were of a somewhat unpleasant description, owing to a misunderstanding he had with a so-called Young Men's *Christian* Association; it arose thus :- Two committee men had been negotiating to secure him. The Y. M. C. A. committee telegraphed Mr. Wilde's agent, offering $75 for a lecture on Friday night. Mr. Husted answered that terms were satisfactory for

---

[10] *The Century*, for November, 1882, contains an exquisitely humorous poem by Helen Gray Cone, describing an imaginary interview between Oscar Wilde and the great poetical Egotist - Walt Whitman. The style and diction of both are admirably hit off, better perhaps (because easier to catch) is the parody of Whitman, which reads, indeed, like an excerpt from his works.

The poem concludes thus :-

Narcissus.   What more is left to say or do?
Our minds have met; our hands must part.
I go to plant in pastures new,
The love of Beauty and of Art.
I'll shortly start.
One town is rather small for two
Like me and you!

Thursday night and requested a reply. This was about 4 p.m. At about 8 p.m., four hours later, the Y. M. C. A. committee replied that Thursday night was satisfactory. Mr. Wilde then replied in effect: "Waited till 7; then had to close with other parties. Sorry." Another committee of townspeople had in the meantime closed with Mr. Wilde. Then the Y. M. C. A. obtained a writ which was served on Mr. Wilde. The Y. M. C. A. laid damages at $200. Mr. Husted offered to give them $20 and pay costs. This was not accepted. Finally Mr. Estey and Mr. Weldon gave bonds for $500 for Mr. Wilde's appearance. The action of the Y. M. C. A. people is generally condemned in the colony, both the very pious, who lift up their eyes and hands in pious horror at one who attempts to raise the love of Art and Beauty into a kind of religious worship; and by the ungodly, who see that the Y. M. C. A. merely sought to fill its coffers out of the attraction of this Arch Prophet, irrespective of his teachings, and failing in that, feed their revenge by attempts to levy black mail.

It is probable that on his return from American he will publish an account of his experiences; such a volume could not fail to prove interesting, as he has visited every city, has seen every sight of interest or importance, and has been received and entertained by nearly every man of eminence in art or letters, to say nothing of the interviews he has had with the reporters of nearly every important transatlantic newspaper.

In his highly successful lecture on "Art Decoration," Oscar Wilde, after deprecating the common error of multiplying designs by machine work, as in wall papers, carpets, &c., reverts to the peculiarly ugly nature of men's dress as at present worn, advocating the use of flowing robes or drapery, and brighter colours than are in fashion now.

On the not unimportant topic of dress there are few men who would deny that the costume they wear is at once ugly and uncomfortable, but they would sadly urge that deference to usage and conventionality compels them to retain it.

Oscar Wilde defies conventionality, and has set a fashion of garb which one might well wish to be universally adopted. Yet, alas! what suits *his* figure might not in all its details be adapted for the every-day wear of ordinary mortals of less heroic proportions and statuesque form. To begin with the *hat*; the tall hat is becoming a few countenances, and how eager we all are to exchange it for a polo cap or a deer-stalker, or any other form less heavy, more yielding to the brow, and less attractive to the heat in the sun. Tennyson goes about in a wide-brimmed felt hat, a "swart sombrero" it is indeed - and bears a cloak almost toga-like in its proportions.

The *toga* might be hard to manage on a windy day, but knee-breeches and stockings, or tall boots, would surely be more sightly and far more comfortable than the loose ends of trousers flapping round one's ankles and catching all the mud. Why are we for ever to be tied up in black frock or cutaway coats, a velvet or cloth tunic like those worn by the converted dragoons in *Patience* would be far more comfortable, and more comely.

But, indeed, we well know what is the more comfortable; it is the garb that most men assume when out for pleasure, one that interferes least with the actions and movements of the body; and somewhat *modified* as to *colour* and *texture*, there is no good reason why men should not adopt a similar costume for their daily avocations to what they now wear when boating, riding, or bicycling. The gain in comfort, appearance, and economy, would be great indeed.

Mr. Wilde's exertions in this direction are certainly praiseworthy, and if he can succeed in banishing tall hats, black frock coats, stand-up collars and loose trousers, the world will owe him a vast debt of gratitude.

In this matter he is not alone, for of late many people have been raising an outcry in favour of rationalism in dress, both for men and women, and Mr. J. Alfred Gotch, in his pamphlet styled "Art in Costume" (published by Kegan, Paul and Co., London) has most effectively backed up Oscar Wilde's views in favour of soft low-crowned hats, jackets, knee breeches, and stockings, either with or without high boots, according to the season.

Mr. Gotch pleads for the sake of comfort, utility and economy, Mr. Wilde for the sake of Beauty. It rarely happens that such various attributes can be so surely reconciled and brought together as in this agitation for a reform in Dress.

Mr. O. Wilde is a brilliant conversationalist, a happy one too in many senses, for he can listen as well as he can talk, and he can talk so that listening to his conversation, even to the garrulous, becomes more pleasant than to listen to their own.

He speaks enthusiastically about the reception accorded to him in the States, where he was entertained by poets, such as Longfellow and Wendell Holmes, where his lectures were crowded, his photographs sold in enormous numbers, and crowds were in waiting even at small roadside stations to catch a glimpse of him. He found that the masses on the American continent were much better educated than they were in England.

Several sketches of Mr. Wilde have appeared in the American journals, one, especially good, with critical notes on the poems, was given in *The Salt Lake Journal*.

It is said that shortly after his return to London, Mr. Wilde intends to set out for a trip to Japan, with a view to studying art as it exists in that singular country, art indeed to which much that is really Aesthetic has been frequently compared - we shall know on his return with how much justice and accuracy.

Botticelli and E. Burne-Jones, Oxford and Japan, *Romeo and Juliet* at the Lyceum Theatre and *Patience* at the Savoy, Wagner and Sullivan, Swinburne and Oscar Wilde; how widely asunder do these all sound, how dissimilar their attributes, yet each and all in a manner aggregate to form the Aesthetic School, and have helped it to the position it holds at present, high in the estimation of all true lovers of the ideal, the passionate, and the beautiful.

A HOME FOR THE AESTHETES

YE HAUNTED HOUSE.
By Raymond H. Phillimore.)
I knowe a house at Turnham Greene,
　　Fayre Syr, I knowe yt well;
Yt ys a house where men rejoyce,
　　And Fyerie spyrrytes dwell;
A trumpeter hee swings wythont,
　　Hys name I cannot tell.

"Who lyeth there?" Thou ask'st mee that?
　　Ye Parsonne? Saye not soe;
Hee loveth not ye house I mean
　　To yt hee wyll not goe;
For holie men they haunt yt not,
　　And soe I answere "Noe."

Ye spyrrytes dwellynge there are goode,
　　Yet leade they some to synne;
Thou ask'st theyre names? I tell thee true;
　　They call them Brandie, Gynne;
Fayre Syr, yt ys a ryghte goode house,
　　Yt ys ye "Tabarde" Inne.

Turnham Greene,
　　Ye Fyrst daye of Maye,
　　　MDCCCLXXXII.

"Your book on the Aesthetic School will never be complete without a description of the Bedford Park Estate," said a friend to me; so I took a train from the Mansion House station, and in less than half an hour was landed on the sunny platform of the Turnham Green and Bedford Park station.

As it was just about lunch time, I made at once for *The Tabard*, a noted hostelry, which had been recommended to my notice by the aforesaid friend, whose interest in the Aesthetic Movement is "intense," and to whom I am indebted for much information about it.

Well, I easily found *The Tabard*, for it is only about two minutes' walk from the station; outside, it is true, there was nothing to indicate that it was a tavern except a very handsomely-painted signboard, representing on one side a Court Herald wearing an embroidered *Tabard* (that is a short coat such as knights used to wear over their armour, with their arms emblazoned on it), and on the other an old-fashioned inn, having also the Tabard for a sign. In other respects the house was similar in general appearance to most of those around, build of bright red brick in the Queen Anne style, that

> "Age of Lustre and of Link
> Of Chelsea china and long S'es,
> Of Bagwigs and flowered Dresses -
> That age of Folly and of Cards,
> Of Hackney Chairs and Hackney Bards."

There was a good deal of wood work, square windows with small panes of coloured glass, and a general air of warmth and old English comfort about it.

Lunch finished, I rambled about the rooms of *The Tabard*. Everything was quite in keeping with its exterior style - wall-papers, carpets, carved work, tiled fireplaces, all of the early

English and most pronounced Aesthetic type, and to my mind thoroughly tasteful in their soft, subdued colours and quint old-fashioned look.

Even its name has an antique sound, for was it not from the *Tabard Inn*, in the Borough, that Chaucer's pilgrims started on their memorable journey to Canterbury five hundred years ago? Whilst examining the large room over the bar I was joined by the manager, Mr. Lemberger, who courteously directed my attention to many points of interest. Amongst other things, I had a close view of the signboard, which is a veritable work of art. It was painted by Mr. Rooke, A. R. A., at a cost, I was told, of 100 guineas; it certainly appears too handsome and too highly finished to be exposed, as it is, to all weathers.

It seems that glass would be no protection to it, but that about every three months it is varnished with some preservative solution; and certainly its colours do not appear as yet to have lost any of their original brilliancy.

Even in the public bar the old style is imitated, the walls being of sober colour, relieved by painted tiles, and everywhere there is an absence of the garish glitter and the sham splendour of the modern gin-place. Whether the ordinary frequenter of a tavern bar appreciates these artistic refinements is a question we need not now consider; but as the gorgeous fittings of a public-house have to be paid for by the customers in the long run, they would be wise to seek a quiet-looking house if they would have pure unadulterated beverages.

But at Bedford Park there is not much choice in the matter, for the *Tabard* appears to be the only inn on the estate; next door to it are the Stores amply supplied with every domestic necessity, opposite is the Church, and a little way up the street is the Art

School, all of which are built and furnished on the same general principles. But the Club is undoubtedly the most attractive feature at Bedford Park.

The exterior of the building is so plain and simple that it might easily be taken for a gentleman's residence. Inside I found comfort and elegance, without ostentation; books, flowers, and pictures, china and glass ornaments were scattered about, and a general air of cosiness and warmth pervaded the rooms; whilst - through the open casements - views of the sunlit lawn, the hawthorn trees in full bloom, golden laburnum and sweetly-scented lilac could be seen, and the gentle splashing of a fountain only served to make the delicious quiet and repose of the surroundings more apparent; of some such dwelling it must have been that Thomson sang :-

> "Was nought around but images of rest;
> Sleep-soothing groves, and quiet lawns between;
> And flowery beds that slumbrous influence kest,
> From poppies breath'd; and beds of pleasant green,
> Where never yet was creeping creature seen.
> Meantime, unnumber'd glittering streamlets play'd,
> And buried everywhere their waters sheen;
> That, as they bicker'd through the sunny glade,
> Though restless still themselves, a lulling murmur made.
>
> A pleasing land of drowsy head it was,
> Of dreams that wave before the half-shut eye;
> And of gay castles in the clouds that pass,
> For ever flushing round a summer sky.
> There eke the soft delights, that witchingly
> Instil a wanton sweetness through the breast,

And the calm pleasures always hover'd night;

But whate'er smack'd of noyance, or unrest,

Was far, far off expell'd from this delicious nest."

But I am getting discursive.

From an attendant I obtained a list of the rules of the club, which told me that it was formed as a means of affording social intercourse for the residents of the Bedford Park Estate, and their friends.

The club contains billiard, reading and card rooms, and the prettiest of all possible ladies' drawing-rooms. All the principal newspapers and magazines are taken in, there is a small library, and new books are constantly supplied by the Grosvenor Gallery Library.

The internal decorations of the club are, of course, in the Early English style, and indeed much of the furniture is truly antique, the book-shelves and settees being of finely carved oak of the 17th century; whilst other pieces are of the dark perforated carved work formerly made in India.

The large hall is beautifully decorated; the old panels, with classical subjects worked in gold on ebony, which fill the wall space over the mantelboard, are especially noticeable. It is in this hall that the theatrical entertainments take place, for which a small neat stage is fitted up. Concerts, lectures, and other amusements are frequently given, also fancy dress balls, in which, it is said, the costumes show much taste and variety, the artistic inhabitants having here an opportunity to display their skill in design and colour.

These are a few of the inducements held out to residents to join the club, at the enormous annual outlay of two guineas, (half a guinea only in the case of a lady); then there are concerts in the large room, monthly dinners, dances and dramatic performances.

Outside the club there is a lawn tennis ground, pleasantly shaded by handsome trees, it adjoins and overlooks the beautiful gardens belonging to the Tower House, the residence of Mr. Carr, the proprietor of the estate.

The little colony of Bedford Park had no existence, even in the imagination of its enthusiastic proprietor, until within the last six or seven years, before which time the site selected by Mr. Carr for his experiment did not differ from the surrounding country.

The monotony of a continuous prospect of fields and orchards, was being gradually invaded and encroached upon by long dreary rows of brick and stucco houses of the Pimlico type, so dear to the speculative builder, who can build street upon street in this type without any exercise in his ingenuity, except as to how best to utilize his old materials, rejected bricks, mortar destitute of binding power, doors that refuse to open, and windows which it is impossible to shut; roofs which let in the water, and drains which will not carry it away; deep dismal basements, meant only for the home of the beetle and cockroach, and huge flights of pretentious stone steps for people to slip down in frosty weather, and for poor servants to kneel at for hours to white stone over. But here, at Bedford Park, a good fairy seems to have been at work, and the view from the railway is brightened by an oasis amidst the surrounding desert of stereotyped suburban settlements.

This result is due to the enterprise of Mr. Jonathan Carr, who originated the idea, in which he has been ably assisted by his architect, Mr. R. Norman Shaw, and although for a time the scheme was laughed at as Utopian and absurd, it has long since passed into the stage of a recognized success, and fast as the houses are being built, the demand is ahead of the supply.

Whilst admitting the credit due to Mr. Carr for the initiative he has taken in the matter, it must be conceded that he started with several elements of success in his favour.

First of all was the undoubted revival in artistic taste which has been making its way amongst the well-to-do middle class of English people since the Exhibition of 1851; next came the important fact that Mr. Carr was the possessor of a plot of land admirably adapted by nature for such a retreat as he has turned it into, and of all its natural beauties he has taken the fullest advantage, the wide avenues being lined with some of the finest old trees to be found near London.

Again, whilst being sufficiently removed from the noise, smoke, and bustle of London, it is not so far distant as to prevent City men from making it their home, or ladies from taking those pleasant but costly journeys to town, known to husbands as "going shopping." And for all these journeys, whether for business or pleasure, every facility of conveyance is near at hand.

So taking all these natural advantages into consideration, Mr. Carr determined that the architecture and arrangements of the colony should be in keeping with its surroundings, and in harmony with the artistic taste of the period.

To have built only a few houses in the exceptional style he had planned out would have been costly beyond all possibility of remunerative return, but by laying out the buildings in groups of detached and semi-detached houses somewhat similar in their *main features*, but exceedingly varied in *matters of detail*, the objection of excessive expense was removed, and the houses, with all their advantages, are let at rents no higher than those of the dreary roads and streets of Pimlico, or Camden-town.

One great charm of the idea is, that no two houses are exactly alike, and the picturesque aspect of the whole makes one marvel that the idea is so novel, especially when the feeling will keep rising in one's mind, that it is a little piece of an old English town which has somehow or another escaped the ravages of time, to show us how much more sensible our ancestors were, in some respects, than we who live in this much-vaunted nineteenth century.

This illusion is made all the more perfect from the pains that have been taken not to spoil the rural appearance of the estate - not a tree has been needlessly cut down; each house is sheltered, many are perfectly embowered in jasmine, laburnum, and hawthorn, and the aspect of the avenues, on a sunny day, is full of such old-world repose, colour and sweetness as even Tennyson could describe, or Ruskin could desire.

Healthy air, a gravel soil, the rive near enough for those who love boating, charming walks around, Kew Gardens only distant by a ten minutes ride by rail, and the great world of London but half an hour away. And yet what need to wander away; are there not the club and the theatre, the church and the *Tabard?* Even shopping can be done, and comfortably, too, on the estate, for at the Stores nearly every requisite of civilized life can be obtained, and for all practical purposes Bedford Park is a little world in itself. As one wanders along the avenues, under the gently rustling trees, the sunlight wavers and flickers on the red brick fronts of the houses; many of the doors are open, and the neat halls are visible with their clean cool Indian matting, square old-fashioned brass lamps; comfort and elegance everywhere, lightness and grace abound. Even the names on the door-posts have a touch of poetry and quaintness about them :- Pleasaunce, Elm-dene, Kirk Lees, Ye Denne, for example.

Nearly every house has also a balcony, not the ordinary kind of iron abomination jutting out like a huge wart on the face of the house, and dangerous even for children to stand upon, but a good sized square comfortable arrangement, generally forming the roof of some out-building, surrounded with a low parapet, and affording a pleasant view of the trees and gardens around - the place of all others to sit in the hot summer evenings, to smoke a cigar, and play a quiet game of chess. How Thackeray, with his love for the Queen Anne style, would have delighted in the view to be obtained from any of these buildings; what a "Round-about Paper" he would have written on the reminiscences it called up of Addison Steele, and *The Spectator.*

The great charm about the estate is the absence of conventionality; there is none of the usual dull monotony about the exterior of the houses, the roads wind about without any apparent desire to lead anywhere in particular, or of having any intention of returning when they get there. They are sheltered by pleasant trees, and are not bordered by dismal rows of cast iron railings all moulded on the same pattern. Low wooden fences mark the boundaries of the gardens, and allow one to see over and admire the trim parterres full of Nature's brightest jewellery. Wood, brick, or stone show for what they are, and do not make absurd and ineffectual attempts to look like ebony, or marble, or terra cotta. There is no stucco, no gilt, no affectation, no monotony; but there is comfort, cleanliness, taste, green trees, and plenty of fresh air.

Tower House stands at the corner of two charming avenues, and whilst one of the largest residences on the estate, is far more noticeable for the beauty of its internal fittings and furniture, than for its external appearance, which is, in front at least, somewhat more simple than its neighbours, but the garden face and the grounds themselves are very pretty.

Availing myself of the courteous invitation of Mrs. Carr to look over her house, I was delighted with the exquisite taste displayed in it. The hall, dining-room, and drawing-room, all on the entrance floor, are large and well lit, whilst the staircase with its wide stairs and massive banisters remind one of the old-fashioned manor halls still to be found on quiet country estates. The prevailing colours used in the decorations are soft neutral tints, nothing brilliant or startling being seen. The projecting windows are fitted with large square casements, comfortable window seats and cushions. The walls of the dining-room are panelled with fine old carved oak, most of which was obtained by Mr. Carr from the fittings of an old City church, St. Dionysius Backchurch, an edifice which even the fame of its architect, Sir Christopher Wren, could not save from destruction when its site was required for modern street improvements.

In both the dining and drawing-rooms the floors are of polished wood, not covered with regularly fitting carpets complete, but with Persian or Turkey rugs of various sizes and shapes; in the drawing-room the walls are hung round with some fine pieces of very old tapestry brought by Mr. Carr from Spain, and very valuable paintings; then books, flowers, and pottery form an *ensemble* which it would indeed be hard to match for beauty and originality.

In this style of old English furniture, wall hangings should be largely used, curtains employed in place of folding doors, and the panels of halls and staircases covered with Indian or other matting easily removed and cleansed. For dining and drawing-rooms, tapestry hangings might be used were it not for the extreme costliness of that material.

In the internal decorations of a new house an incoming tenant at Bedford Park has much liberty of selection; the majority of the residents have chosen from the wall-papers and designs furnished by Mr. William Morris, whose establishment at Bloomsbury is extensive enough to supply new and varied patterns without any fear of sameness or monotony in passing from one house in the estate to another. Besides, the changes can so easily be rung when there are dado papers, tiles, or matting, wall-papers, distemper, hangings and tapestry to select from, that the danger of monotony in this new style of decoration is avoided.

Whilst on the subject of the beauty of houses, I am tempted to quote a few paragraphs from an interesting paper by E. Randolph, which appeared in *The Burlington* for last April, describing the decadence of modern domestic architecture.

"It is doubtful whether utilitarian ugliness pure and simple, was ever so characteristic of any race as it was of our immediate forefathers.

"We were not always an ugly people. Mediaeval England was beautiful; Elizabethan splendid; Jacobean quaint and picturesque; a refined elegance marks the modified Dutch and Queen Anne.

"With the Georges, however, came decadence, which is plainly traceable to the influence of the Court: a heavy animation, a plain obtrusive ugliness, for which the best word its defenders had was 'sensible,' prevailed throughout the land.

"What were the minds of those men, for example, who designed and built Gower Street?

"It is true the Londoner has always looked, until lately, to the inside, not the outside of his house; but beauty of any sort at this period was a rarity indeed, and as a rule internals and externals were quite on a par.

"All colour was voted vulgar. In the better parts of London red brick, the most useful and most effective of material, was debarred by law. Art may be said to have languished under a penal code, and universal ugliness reigned supreme with free fell scope. It had its day, and a long day it was; but the reaction came at last. Again the court was splendid, wasteful, extravagant. Decorative art blazed out in all the shabby ostentation of the Regency, which points to the Pavilion at Brighton as its proudest monument. A style of prismatic lustre, stiff cut glass, mirrors, false stones, cheap gilding, barbaric colour and outrageous curve of vast facades in lath and plaster; it was a veritable apotheosis of stucco, a pageant and triumph of sham!

"After this pyrotechnic display, art in this country sank down into its ashes, and for a time expired altogether. With art ecclesiastical we are not concerned at present, but during the reigns of the four Georges it may be said to have been nil, as the few and melancholy restorations, and still fewer and more melancholy erections of that period sufficiently prove."

One of the most imposing-looking buildings on the estate is the Chiswick School of Art, a red brick house, with quaint gables, and projecting windows full of small panes of glass. A large porch, with handsome doors glazed with coloured glass, opens into the hall, right and left of which are two fine classrooms, over these again are two, still larger. In one room when I entered, the pupils were drawing from models; in another they were painting, and one young lady was just putting the finishing touches to a very life-like representation of that aesthetic favourite, that bright emblem of constancy - the brilliant sunflower.

I noticed, too, that in many instances the young ladies were decidedly of the aesthetic type, both as to the mode of dress, and fashion of arranging their hair.

The building seems admirably designed for its purposes, the rooms being lofty and well lit; and in its decorations and artistic appliances, there appears to be every incentive to the art student to learn to love the beautiful, and to realise the ideal.

This building was from the designs of Mr. Maurice B. Adams, A. R. I. B. A., who is also hon. secretary of the School of Art, which is in connection with the Science and Art Department, South Kensington; there are on the Committee the names of some of the most influential residents in Bedford Park, and the classes are even now largely attended, although the school has not long been in operation.

The fees are very moderate, and the subjects of study include freehand drawing, geometry and perspective, architectural and mechanical drawing, painting in oil and water colours, studies from the human figure, decorative art, as applied to wall-papers, furniture, metal-work, stained glass, &c., &c.

Art needlework, pottery, tile painting, and etching will also be included before long.

Numerous scholarships and prizes are open to the art students, so that there is no lack of encouragement, and in these days, when the fine arts are becoming more and more appreciated and understood, it is difficult to over-estimate the intellectual advantages young people are likely to derive from such tuition, or the great social and pecuniary success they may obtain.

But whilst individuals are reaping these special benefits, however much greater will be the national gain from the gradual dissemination of the canons of true taste, in the harmony and blending of colours, in the design of forms for various purposes possessing not only the requisite strength and solidity, but also as much beauty of form as is consistent with the material and the other requisites of work and durability.

Whilst the study of colours has had, and will have, a great effect upon clothing and furniture, that of the beauty of form should be particularly commended to our architects and engineers, for all foreign critics, whilst admitting the strength and solidity of English buildings, bridges, and machinery, find fault with their heavy, sombre, and inelegant appearance.

William Morris, when speaking on the recent improvement in knowledge of art, says it is no use to trust to the rich and fashionable for a revival of true decorative art. They, he says -

"have no chance of spending time enough over the arts to know anything practical of them, and they must of necessity be in the hands of those who can spend most time in pushing a fashion this or that way for their own advantage.

"There is no help to be got out of these latter, or those who let themselves be led by them; the only real help for the decorative arts must come from those who work in them; nor must they be led; they must lead.

"You whose hands make those things that should be works of art, you must be all artists, and good artists, before the public at large can take real interest in such things; and when you have become so, I promise you that you shall lead the fashion; fashion shall follow your hands obediently enough.

"There is a great deal of sham work in the world, hurtful to the buyer, more hurtful to the seller, if only he knew it, most hurtful to the maker; how good a foundation it would be toward getting good decorative art - that is, ornamental workmanship - if we craftsmen were to resolve to turn out nothing but excellent workmanship in all things, instead of having, as we too often have now, a very low average standard of work, which we often fall below."

Such, in brief, is the teaching of the masters of the new school. Ruskin's volumes all tend in the same direction. Away with all shams; study pure art purely for art's sake; avoid false gold and pretentious glitter; adopt a simple style moulded on the forms and colours of nature.

CONCLUSION

THE SEVEN STAGES OF AESTHETICISM.

All the world's aesthetic,
And all the men and women merely aesthetes;
They have their yearnings and their ecstasies;
And each man in his time plays many parts,
His acts being seven stages. First, the Philistine,
Sneering at Art's high transcendental charms;
And next the clinging Pupil, with his lily
And elongated chin, sliding like snake
To study in the school. Then, the Acolyte,
Sighing like furnace, with a woeful sonnet
Made to a dado. Then, the full-fledged Poet,
Full of strange whims, long-haired as Absalom,
Jealous of fame, profuse of attitude,
Seeking the bubble reputation
E'en at the tea-pot's spout. Then, the Professor,
With bilious mien, and clothes not wisely cut,
His monologues quite too idealised,
Bursting with Culture, and the Infinite;
And so he plays his part. The sixth stage shifts
Into the lank and velvet-suited Humbug,
With nippers on his nose and tuft on his chin;
His mystic style, well saved, a world too wide
For his shrunk audience; while his croaky voice,
Striving again to rouse to rapture, seems
But senseless in its sound. Last scene of all,

That ends this strange eventful history,

Is the utter idiocy and mere oblivion,

Sans mind, sans taste, sans Art, sans everything.

The worst feature of the present age is, that it is the fashion to treat nothing seriously but folly, to sneer at every one who is in earnest, no matter on what topic, and a silly parody like the above will often carry more conviction than would a serious criticism invoking some little thought and consideration.

Much of the merriment is forced, and few of the jests are original, but it is so much easier to jeer at the teachings of a philosopher, than to understand or to profit by them.

In France, this habit of trifling with all serious topics had already led the people into grievous trouble, and in England it is gradually undermining the sober solidity of the national character.

Many men would rather stifle their enthusiasm and hide their talents, than become the butt of the silly buffoons who have the ear of the public, but who can only parody and distort the utterances of the poet, or the philosopher.

The vitality of Aestheticism could not have been better proved than in its power to survive the sarcasms and the ridicule to which it has been subjected ever since it first came into notice. How small, how insignificant, indeed, the names *now* appear of the men identified with these attacks, as compared with those of the leaders of Aestheticism, now also generally acknowledged as our chiefs in painting and poetry, the dramatic and decorative arts.

And these have chosen three emblems, not fortuitously nor unthinkingly, but of a set purpose we may surely suppose. Purity, Beauty, and Constancy: are they not adequately expressed to the mind's eye, as also to the eyes with which we merely see externals, in the lily, the peacock, and the sun-flower. Cheap derision skims but the surface, and finds matter for a sorry sneer, or pitiful jest, in things which to the observant and the thoughtful are pregnant with deep meaning and suggestive pathos. In the first verse of his first poem, Dante Rossetti introduced the lily-purity :-

> "The blessed damozel leaned out
>   From the gold bar of Heaven;
> Her eyes were deeper than the depth
>   Of waters stilled at even;
> She had three lilies in her hand,
>   And the stars in her hair were seven."

So he, too, great lover of the beautiful, found a world of glowing colour in the feathers of that bird, which our forefathers se greatly prized for its stately grandeur, and its lovely plumage; how gloriously, too, it decks the background of many a grand mediaeval landscape, strutting majestically along the sunlit avenues; as, indeed, it does in some of the modern paintings of the so-called Pre-Raphaelite artists, notably in one by Arthur Hughes, his sweetly-suggestive "Silver and Gold." And for the sun-flower that ever turns its glowing face towards the Lord of light and love, hath it not perfection of form and colour in its circles of black and gold to recommend it, irrespective of its poetical *Je vous suis partout* character. Deny it all these attributes, it is still worthy of a better fate than to be derided of the Philistines.

Is it not worshipped by the Chinese, most utilitarian of people, and well does it merit the homage they render it, for it is the most useful of all vegetables. From its seeds is made a lubricant oil, and soap unequalled for softening the skin. Sunflower oil burns longer than any other vegetable oil. Sunflower cake is more fattening than linseed cake, its flowers supply the best bee food, and its leaves are used as a substitute for tobacco. Its stalk yields a fine fibre used in Chinese silk, and the best yellow dies of the Chinese are produced from its flowers.

It has occurred to some ingenious and erudite persons that it would appear very learned, and witty, to compare the Aesthetic School of Poetry to that which was known, about eighty years ago, as the *Della Cruscan* school.

But whereas the Della Cruscans produced no poetry which has survived even till now, the poems of Swinburne, Morris, and Rossetti, will last as long as our language is read. Again, the Della Cruscans had not enough vitality to survive the one bold vigorous onslaught of Gifford in his *Baviad and Maeviad*, but were laughed right out of existence, whereas *Aestheticism* which has long been spitefully abused and misrepresented, is to-day in all its essentials, more vigorous than ever; its poems are more widely read, its dictates in all matters of taste are more generally adopted, and O think it may safely be predicted that the poetry of the Aesthetic School will come to be regarded as a distinct growth typical of the later half of the nineteenth century, as the Lake School of Poetry was of the earlier portion.

The Lake writers have outlived the scorn of their contemporaries, and in the same way people will live to see how much there is of the good, the beautiful, and the true, in the Aesthetic Movement, and to recognize the beneficial influence it has had upon modern life in the cultivation of good taste in art.

In the *Burlington* for July last, there appeared an able paper, entitled "A Plea for Aestheticism;" it very clearly pointed out some of the benefits we have derived from the movement, and the following paragraphs are worthy of the consideration of those even who dislike and ridicule the school :-

"Under different names the irregular recurrence of an aesthetic movement - that is to say, the aspiration of a select few to a higher culture than that of the many - has been a peculiar feature in the social history of the modern world.

"Most people's knowledge of the Précieuses is wholly derived from Molière's two plays, in which they cut so ludicrous a figure; but to regard these as pictures of the society of the Hôtel de Rambouillet is about as logical as to accept the caricatures of Du Maurier, Burnand, and Gilbert, as faithful representations of the aesthetic movement, which, indeed, ninety-nine people out of every hundred really do. As a matter of course, ignorant imitators and silly fanatics, such as Molière has depicted, identified themselves with the movement, and provided food for the satirists, who did not care to weaken the point of their satire by discriminating between the true and the false apostles.

"From the age of Louis XIV. to that of Napoleon III. France was the model to Europe in the polish of its manners, the elegance of its language, and the perfection of its taste, and for all these advantages it was indebted to the Précieuses. Like the aesthetes of to-day, they brought about a vast reform in the aspect of their domestication; they studied elegance of form, and harmony of colour and natural beauty in decorations; they instituted the Académie, and they taught men and women that grace of manner which, once upon a time, rendered the title of lady or gentleman a true mark of distinction that could not be indiscriminately applied.

"Yet for all these benefits the Précieuses have descended to prosperity only as certain half-crazy and absurd personages, who rendered themselves laughing stocks in their day, and were ultimately extinguished by the ridicule of common-sense people. It will be much the same with the aesthetes; our great-grandsons will turn over the leaves of antique volumes of *Punch*, and students of old dramatic literature will peruse *The Colonel* and *Patience*, and wonder how people could be so ridiculous, utterly ignoring the fact that the cultured taste which appears in their homes, from a kitchen utensil to a carpet and wall-paper and a lady's dress, and which contrasts so marvellously with the barbaric horrors of the early Victorian era, over which he has laughed in other antique caricatures, were the work of these so-called ridiculous people.

"Indeed the inconsistencies of posterity are already anticipated. Mrs. Philistine Jones pays a visit to the Savoy, or the Prince of Wales's, enjoys the satire, and wonders how people can make such fools of themselves as to be aesthetic. Now a dozen years ago Mrs. Jones would have appeared at the theatre in a costume hideous in form, and utterly discordant in colour, instead of which she now wears a dress with, at least, some pretensions to artistic design and the blending of harmonious tints. To whom is she indebted for the change? Why, to 'the fools,' for whom she expressed such disdain. Mr. Philistine Jones dubs all the aesthetes idiots, while he also adopts their ideas. A dozen years ago his dazzling carpets and wall-papers were enough to give a good templar a fit of delirium tremens; his furniture was a roughly hewn mass of ponderous mahogany; his walls were hung with abominations, encircled in tawdry gilt frames, which he called pictures; he delighted in waxen fruit under glass covers; his crockery, his glass - in fine, everything he possessed, and especially what he admired - was a violation of good taste. But somehow he has changed all this; the human eye may now repose upon the neutral tints of his carpets and walls. He has even a dado, and blue china may be espied in nooks and corners; he has eschewed gilt, and his pictured and ornaments no longer excite in you iconoclastic desires; he has ceased to care for stucco; he lives in a Queen Anne house, and actually has begun to think something about the shape of his jugs.

"This improvement is rapidly spreading through all classes of society - good taste is no longer an expensive luxury to indulge in - the commonest articles of domestic use are now fashioned in accordance with its laws, and the poorest may have within their homes, at the cost of a few pence, cups and saucers and jugs and teapots, more artistic in form and design than were to be found twenty years ago in any homes but those of the cultured rich.

"And to whom are we indebted for these advantages? Why, to the Aesthetes, the fools and idiots of Philistine phraseology."

Those persons who are inclined to undervalue the labours of the so-called Aesthetic School (a term I have employed only because it is generally used, and not because I think it either correct, or expressive), would do well to seriously revise their judgement upon what has really been affected by those belonging to the higher range of Aestheticism.

There must be some good in a theory, or system, initiated and worked out by men of such eminence in art, as Holman Hunt, E. Burne-Jones, and Walter Crane; in art and poetry combined, as D. G. Rossetti, Thomas Woolner, and Morris; in poetry and criticism by such as A. C. Swinburne, William M. Rossetti, John Ruskin, and Oscar Wilde. But let it be borne in mind that higher Aestheticism has nothing in common with the affected and superficial Aestheticism which has been forced into a hot house existence by caricaturists, and fostered by those who mistake artistic slang, and stained-glass attitudes, for culture and high art. For herein lies the essence of it all :- Real culture is a hardy plant, it will thrive where it has once taken root; *pseudo*-Aestheticism may for a time be confounded with it by those who have learnt all they know of it from *Punch* and *Patience*, but assuredly by no others, and it will fade away as rapidly as it sprang into existence, with all the more speed now that as a theme for comic writers it is nearly exhausted.

With pure Aestheticism, as with Pre-Raphaelitism, the case is altogether different. Here we have something tangible, which deserves to live as a noble outcome of modern intellect striving to realise a lofty ideal, and to attain that beauty in Art which abounds in Nature. It was through the writings of Ruskin that thousands became acquainted with the works of those, who, seceding from the dreary routine of the conventional art schools, determined henceforth to follow Nature alone, but I will give it in the Master's own language :-

"Pre-Raphaelitism has but one principle, that of absolute uncompromising truth in all that it does, obtained by working everything, down to the minute detail, from Nature and from Nature only; or, where imagination is necessarily trusted to, by always endeavouring to conceive a fact as it really was likely to have happened, rather than as it *most prettily* might have happened. Every Pre-Raphaelite landscape back-ground is painted to the last touch in the open air, from the thing itself. Every Pre-Raphaelite figure, however studied in expression, is a true portrait of some living person. Every minute accessory is painted in the same manner; this is the main Pre-Raphaelite principle."

Rossetti suggested the name of the P. R. Brotherhood, although, of course, the principle involved had existed before, but it had fallen into disuse, and art was nearly suffocated beneath the restrictions imposed upon it by the schools, and the professors, who wished to reduce it to a mere science.

So also in Aestheticism there is much that is old, as old indeed as are beauty and truth, simplicity and grace; and as Ruskin deemed it necessary thirty years ago to enter a protest on behalf of the Pre-Raphaelites, to show how their aims were misunderstood, and their genius unappreciated, so I, in a plain homely way, have sought to point out the good there is in the modern artistic revival, known as the Aesthetic Movement. It has already wrought much in the improved taste shown in poetry and painting, in dress, furniture, and house decoration; there is still much for it to achieve. It must teach us to avoid the weary life-struggle that we wage to appear richer than we are, and to live up to means we do not possess. Let us not wear paste if we cannot afford diamonds, and if gold is beyond our means, let us be too proud to indulge in gilt sham. Some of us, *Mr. Punch* amongst the number, would be better and wiser not to ridicule intellectual aims we do not understand, an not to be continually airing an acquaintance we do *not* possess with dukes and duchesses.

But as Thackeray, the greatest of *Punch* writers, himself has said,

Parasites exist alway.

Lightning Source UK Ltd.
Milton Keynes UK

178743UK00001B/288/P